JN327213

英語の師匠
オーガ&セイン Present

TOEIC® テスト攻略トントンメソッド 【Book 1】

銅メダルコース

400点〜600点レベル

大賀リヱ　デイビッド・セイン
Alan Gleason　Bill Benfield　Terry Browning

南雲堂

TOEICなんてこわくない！

何故こわくないのか。別にキャッチフレーズとして唱えている訳ではなくて，私は心からそう思っているの。その理由は次の通り。

理由その1　TOEICテストは何回でも受けられるから。

　そう，何回も受けるチャンスがあるというのは，とてもいいことだ。一回限りの生死をかけた日本の大学入試とは違い，何回でも受けられるというのは，気楽なレクリエーションのような気持ちで受けられるということなのだ。東京などでは毎月，他の都市でも頻繁に受けるチャンスがある。1回目は何がなにやらわからないうちに終わるだろう。しかし，そこで**絶対にあきらめてはいけない**。毎回根気よく申し込んで受けているうちに，パチンコにでも行くような気分で（失礼，行かない人にはわからんだろうが）試験場にひょいひょいと出かけて，頭の体操をしてくるようになれる。必ず続けて最低5回は受験しよう。

理由その2　TOEICは君んちの近くで受けられるから。

　朝の，または午後のお散歩のついでに立ち寄る感じで受けられるってこと。受験会場は受験申込者の住所の近くを指定してくれるから，遠くの遠くの訳のわからん袋小路をうろうろして，挙げ句の果てに遅刻などという事にはまずならない。私は**TOEIC**を受ける必要はないのだが（ナーゼカ？），最近の傾向と対策を見るために，ときどき受験する。そのときいつも思うのだが，下駄履きで5分で行ける受験会場なんて，他の試験ではそんなにないのじゃないかなぁ。これはとても嬉しいことだ，などと考えながら，いそいそとその場に向かう。会場では受付のお姉さんまたはお兄さん，ときにおばさん，おじさんたちが「こんにちは」と，にっこり笑いかけてくれるから，君もそれに「こんにちは」

とにっこりと笑顔で返そう。そこで受験書類を渡す。これでかなり緊張がほぐれて，ぐっと気が楽になるから，いそいそと試験場に入ることができる。

理由その3　君の手には「トントンメソッド」が

　そして，君が **TOEIC** なんてこわくないと思える最大の理由。それは，当然君は，この英語の達人オーガとセインの「**トントンメソッド**」で学習しているという事実だ。だから，余裕を持って隣近所または受験会場全体を睥睨すべし。ただしあまり早くから会場に入って，あたりを睥睨しすぎると，中にはもっとすごい面構えの猛者や，たいして使っていない参考書を何冊も抱えたりしているようなのもいたりするから（実際こういう輩はただの **TOEIC** オタクが多い），ほどほどの時間に到着し，ほどほどに見回し，大分頭に栄養が回らなくなった感じの男女や，新卒らしき者たちがオドオドと鉛筆をなめたり，枝毛をかじったりしているのを見て優越感を持とう。**黒猫トントンの図太さと，オーガとセインが選び抜いた TOEIC 頻出の語彙と受験メソッドを学んだ君には，もうなにも怖いものはない。**

　がんばれー！

GOOD LUCK AND GO FOR IT!!!

TOEIC® テストの問題形式

TOEIC は，「英語でのコミュニケーション能力」をはかるテストです。マークシート方式の計2時間のテストで，Listening Section と Reading Section の2部に分かれています。

LISTENING SECTION （所要時間45分） 100問

Part 1　Photographs　写真描写問題　10問
1枚の写真について4つの短文が1回だけ放送されます。一番写真と合っていると思われるものを(A)(B)(C)(D)から選びます。
写真中の人物や風景，状景などが文として読まれます。文そのものは難しいものではなく，またほとんどの文は現在形，または現在進行形なので，分かり易い問題が多いです。一番得点しやすいパートと言えるでしょう。

Part 2　Question-Response　応答問題　30問
1つの質問または文と，それに対する(A)(B)(C)の3つの応答が1回だけ放送されます。設問も応答もテストブックにはプリントしてありませんから，ある意味では聞く事だけに集中できるパートです。日常生活やビジネスの場面で，いかに的確に応答できるかを試すパートです。始めの疑問詞と質問のキーワードを捉える ことが正解につながります。

Part 3　Short Conversations　会話問題　30問
2人の会話が1回だけ放送されます。質問は3問です。正しいと思われるものを(A)(B)(C)(D)から選びます。**Part 2** と違い，質問も選択肢もテストブックに印刷されていますから，まず会話が始まる前に3つの質問をさっとスキャンしてキーワードを拾うようにしないとなかなか正答できないでしょう。日常生活，ビジネスの場面でのネイティブな表現などが試されるパートです。

Part 4　Short Talks　説明文問　30問

説明文，指示文，伝言，スピーチなどのアナウンスメントがあり，1回だけ放送されます。質問は3問です。正しいと思われるものを(A)(B)(C)(D)から選びます。**Listening Section** で最難関とされるパートです。質問も選択肢もテストブックに印刷されていますから，**Part 3** と同じくアナウンスメントが始まる前にまずそれをスキャンすることが大切です。

READING SECTION（所要時間75分）　100問

Part 5　Incomplete Sentences　短文穴埋め問題　40問
語彙と文法に関する問題が出題されます。文中の空欄に適当と思われる語を(A)(B)(C)(D)から選びます。短時間で40問こなさなければなりませんから，1つの問題に留まらないこと。

Part 6　Text Completion　長文穴埋め問題　12問
Part 5 と同じく語彙と文法に関する問題ですが，手紙，メモなどの文書の中に3つのブランクがあり，それぞれ(A)(B)(C)(D)から正しいと思われる答えを選びます **Part 5** と違って長文なので，ある程度の文脈を理解する必要がありますが，全文を読む時間はないので，宛名，差出人，用件の項を読み，ブランクの前後を読んで解答していきましょう。

Part 7　Reading Comprehension　読解問題　48問
　　　　　Single passage　　1つの文書　28問
　　　　　Double passage　　2つの文書　20問
手紙，新聞記事，公文書，オフィスメモ，Eメール，広告，指示文などの文書を読んで(A)(B)(C)(D)から正しいと思われる答を選びます。**READING SECTION** で最難関のパートです。膨大な語彙とたくさんの長文を短時間でこなすためには，まず質問を読んで，その答えになるキーワードを本文中でスキャンして見つけることです。

Shadowing をしながら語彙を覚えよう！

Shadowing でネイティブな英語を身につけよう。

Shadowing（シャドーイング）とは，簡単に言えば，レコーディングされた教材をかけっぱなしにして，ほんのちょっとそれに遅れて声を出しながらついていく方法です。これは，少し練習すればすぐ習慣になり，最終的には，きれいな英語を話せるようになる，最高の方法です。

ネイティブの英語について何回も練習するうちに，
1) 自然に正しい「発音・イントネーション」が丸ごと身に付く。
2) ネイティブがしゃべる英語の後について読むことで，文の構造が自然にわかってくる。
3) 声を出して読むことで，自分の声がもう一度，脳に入って記憶を確定する。
聞き流しの学習法などとは全く違う，一石三鳥の学習法です。

次のステップに従って，さあ，Shadowing をやってみよう。

STEP 1　CDをスタート。本を見ながら一緒に声を出して読んでいく。1ユニットずつ，CDをかけっぱなしで，声を出してついていってください。CDは**絶対に1文ずつ止めないようにしてください。**

STEP 2　頑張ってできるだけしっかりした声で読もう。ついていけないところは「ウーウー」と声を出しているだけでもよいから，**絶対にCDを途中で止めないように。**

STEP 3　CDをかけ，声を出して1ユニットを何回も，**本を閉じて，見なくても，CDをかけるだけで，ついていけるようになるまで**練習しよう。

電車の中のように，声を出すのはちょっとはばかられるなぁというところでは，口の中でモニョモニョと発音しよう。これでも十分君の脳に記憶させる事ができるはず。

オーガがこれまでにやってきた講座では，事実この練習で英文を覚えてしまった人も多かったのだ。この本はマスターするまでは必携だよ。つねに持ち歩いてちょっとした隙(すき)にのぞくことを習慣にしよう。

STEP 4　**答えを見ずに** CD に遅れずついていけるようになったら，そのユニットの **Review Quiz** をしてみよう。
1) タイマーを **1 問につき 20 秒**，20 問あるので 20×20 問＝6 分 40 秒に設定して下さい。漫然と**タイマーなしにテストをしてはいけません**。
2) 途中で辞書を見てはいけません。

STEP 5　制限時間になったらすぐに止めて，解答で答え合わせをし，正解率を **Power Builder Chart** に記入してチェックしよう。(終わらなかった問題は 0 とします)

STEP 6　**合格ラインは 90%**。ここまで達しなかったら，また **STEP 1** からやり直そう。

STEP 7　合格ラインに達した後は，**Review Quiz** の文で **Shadowing** を繰り返そう！　何回でもトライして英文を自分のものにしよう！

この作業にあきたら，ときには好きな音楽をかけながら，その lyrics を Shadowing するのも楽しいよね。**ガンバレー！**

marketのマークがある長文音声は無料でダウンロードできます。
Shadowing で丸ごと習得できればもうこわいものはない!?
market『トントンメソッド』で検索！

TOEIC® テスト攻略 トントンメソッド＜銅メダルコース Book 1＞
Table of Contents

Unit 1-1	人の性格・容姿（1）	11
Unit 1-2	人の感情と行動（1）	13
Unit 1-3	旅行・海外	15
Unit 1-4	報道・マスメディア（1）	17
Unit 1-5	就職・キャリア（1）	19
Review Quiz for Unit 1		21
黒猫トントンのちょっとブレイク 1		25
Unit 2-1	人の性格・容姿（2）	29
Unit 2-2	ボランティア活動	31
Unit 2-3	車・ドライブ	33
Unit 2-4	エコロジー	35
Unit 2-5	ビジネス・基礎編（1）	37
Review Quiz for Unit 2		39
黒猫トントンのちょっとブレイク 2		43
Unit 3-1	人の性格・容姿（3）	47
Unit 3-2	旅行・ホテル	49
Unit 3-3	就職・キャリア（2）	51
Unit 3-4	健康と病気（1）	53
Unit 3-5	ビジネス・基礎編（2）	55
Review Quiz for Unit 3		57
黒猫トントンのちょっとブレイク 3		61
Unit 4-1	人の感情と行動（2）	65
Unit 4-2	報道・マスメディア（2）	67
Unit 4-3	道具・機器	69
Unit 4-4	健康と病気（2）	71
Unit 4-5	ビジネス・基礎編（3）	73
Review Quiz for Unit 4		75
黒猫トントンのちょっとブレイク 4		79

Unit 5-1	日常生活	83
Unit 5-2	エネルギー・発電	85
Unit 5-3	公共交通	87
Unit 5-4	健康と栄養	89
Unit 5-5	ビジネス・基礎編(4)	91
Review Quiz for Unit 5		93
黒猫トントンのちょっとブレイク 5		97

Unit 6-1	家族・人生	101
Unit 6-2	美術・芸術	103
Unit 6-3	外食・レストラン	105
Unit 6-4	政治・選挙	107
Unit 6-5	ビジネス・基礎編(5)	109
Review Quiz for Unit 6		111
黒猫トントンのちょっとブレイク 6		115

Unit 7-1	ショッピング	119
Unit 7-2	天候・災害	121
Unit 7-3	スポーツとゲーム	123
Unit 7-4	農業・農産物	125
Unit 7-5	コンピューターとネット(1)	127
Review Quiz for Unit 7		129
黒猫トントンのちょっとブレイク 7		133

Speed Reading 速読講座 Scanning - Part 1

Unit 8-1	通信・電話	137
Unit 8-2	教育・学校	139
Unit 8-3	食物とクッキング	141
Unit 8-4	製造・工場	143
Unit 8-5	コンピューターとネット(2)	145
Review Quiz for Unit 8		147
黒猫トントンのちょっとブレイク 8		151

Speed Reading 速読講座 Scanning - Part 2

Unit 1-1
人の性格・容姿 (1)

左の欄から言葉を選んで …… を完成しよう！

回数チェック欄

1. 筋金入りのサッカーファン
   ☑☑☑ di....d soccer fans

テーマ・分野別

2. 締まった身体で機敏なテニス選手たち
   ☑☑☐ l..n and ag..e tennis players

最初は赤シートでかくす。

3. 気遣い支えてくれるパートナー
   ☑☐☐ a caring and su......ve partner

4. 乱暴で無礼な不良
   ☐☐☐ a rough and r..e de......nt

5. 感じやすいティーン
   ☐☐☐ a se......e teenager

問題文

お助けリスト（ABC順）
- aggressive
- agile
- courageous
- delinquent
- devoted
- diehard
- lean
- mean
- participants
- rude
- sensible
- sensitive
- splendid
- supportive

6. 良識ある相談員
   ☐☐☐ a se.....e counselor

ヒントです

7. 意地悪ないじめっ子
   ☐☐☐ a m..n bully

8. 超積極的な営業マン
   ☐☐☐ an ag.......e sales person

9. 勇敢で献身的な消防士たち
   ☐☐☐ co.......s and de....d firefighters

10. かっこいいページェントの参加者たち
    ☐☐☐ sp.....d pageant pa........ts

一回で満点を取るより、何回もやってようやく満点を取る人の方が最後は勝つんだよ。その方が頭の中の memory mechanism（記憶装置）にしっかり残るからだ。

Unit 1-1

人の性格・容姿 (1)

左の欄から言葉を選んで......を完成しよう！

1. 筋金入りのサッカーファン
   di....d soccer fans

2. 締まった身体で機敏なテニス選手たち
   l..n and ag..e tennis players

3. 気遣い支えてくれるパートナー
   a caring and su......ve partner

4. 乱暴で無礼な不良
   a rough and r..e de......nt

5. 感じやすいティーン
   a se......e teenager

6. 良識ある相談員
   a se.....e counselor

7. 意地悪ないじめっ子
   a m..n bully

8. 超積極的な営業マン
   an ag.......e sales person

9. 勇敢で献身的な消防士たち
   co.......s and de....d firefighters

10. かっこいいページェントの参加者たち
    sp.....d pageant pa........ts

aggressive
agile
courageous
delinquent
devoted
diehard
lean
mean
participants
rude
sensible
sensitive
splendid
supportive

一回で満点を取るより、何回もやってようやく満点を取る人の方が最後は勝つんだよ。
その方が頭の中の memory mechanism（記憶装置）にしっかり残るからだ。

Unit 1-1

フレーズ1個目から10個目までの答えをチェックしよう！ CD 2

1. **diehard soccer fans**
[dàihá:(r)d]

2. **lean and agile* tennis players**
[ǽdʒ(ə)l] *発音注意。「アジャ(イ)ル」

3. **a caring and supportive partner**
[səpɔ́:rtiv]

4. **a rough and rude delinquent**
[rú:d]　[dilíŋkwənt]

5. **a sensitive teenager**
[sénsətiv]

6. **a sensible counselor**
[sénsəbl]

7. **a mean bully**
[mí:n]　[búli]

8. **an aggressive sales person**
[əgrésiv]

9. **courageous and devoted firefighters**
[kəréidʒəs]　[fáiərfáitərz]

10. **splendid pageant participants**
[spléndɪd]　[pǽdʒənt]

点数チェック

/10　/10　/10　/10　/10　/10　/10　/10　/10　/10

Unit 1-2
人の感情と行動 (1)

左の欄から言葉を選んで……を完成しよう！

11 活発なチアリーダーたち
pe..y cheerleaders

12 誰かに仕返しをする
get e..n with someone

13 下手くそな言い訳する
make a fe...e excuse

14 安堵(あんど)のため息をつく
br....e a sigh of re...f

15 やっぱり考え直す
have se...d th....ts

16 朝の遅刻常習
ch....c morning ta.....ss

17 温かくもてなす雰囲気
ho.......e at.......e

18 彼に恩を返す
return him the fa..r

19 かっこわるいミスをする
make an em.........g mistake

20 町中のうわさになる
become the t..k of the town

atmosphere
breathe
chronic
embarrassing
even
favor
feeble
hospitable
perky
relief
second
talk
tardiness
thoughts

一回で満点を取るより、何回もやってようやく満点を取る人の方が最後は勝つんだよ。その方が頭の中の memory mechanism（記憶装置）にしっかり残るからだ。

Unit 1-2

フレーズ 11 個目から 20 個目までの答えをチェックしよう! CD 3

11 **perky cheerleaders**
[pə́ːrki]

12 **get even with someone**

13 **make a feeble excuse**
[fíːbl]

14 **breathe a sigh of relief**
[bríːð]

15 **have second thoughts**
[θɔ́ːts]

16 **chronic morning tardiness**
[kránik]

17 **hospitable atmosphere**
[ǽtməsfìər]

18 **return him the favor**
[féivər]

19 **make an embarrassing mistake**
[embǽrəsíŋ]

20 **become the talk of the town**

点数チェック

/10 /10 /10 /10 /10 /10 /10 /10 /10 /10

Unit 1-3

旅行・海外

左の欄から言葉を選んで……を完成しよう！

21 切符は先着順に販売します。
Tickets are sold on a first-c..e first-se...d basis.

22 遺失物取り扱い窓口
the l..t-and-f...d window

23 旅程表を作る
arrange the iti.....y

24 荷物の預かり券
a cl..m-check for the baggage

advisories
apologize
attention
claim
come
delay
destination
found
frequent
itinerary
lost
obtain
served
sightseeing
tourism

25 頻繁利用客へのおまけマイレージ・ポイント
fr.....t-flyer bonus points

26 遅延を詫びる
ap......e for the d...y

27 旅行情報に注意しよう
pay at......n to travel ad.......s

28 最終目的地
final port of de........n

29 観光ビザをとる
ob...n a si........g visa

30 観光業を振興する
foster more to....m

一回で満点を取るより，何回もやってようやく満点を取る人の方が最後は勝つんだよ。その方が頭の中の memory mechanism（記憶装置）にしっかり残るからだ。

Unit 1-3

フレーズ 21 個目から 30 個目までの答えをチェックしよう！　　CD 4

21 Tickets are sold on a first-come first-served basis.
[béisis]

22 the lost-and-found window
[fáund]

23 arrange the itinerary
[aitínərèri]

24 a claim-check for the baggage
[kléim]

25 frequent-flyer bonus points
[frikwént]

26 apologize for the delay
[əpálədʒàiz]

27 pay attention to travel advisories
[ədváizəriːz]

28 final port of destination
[dèstənéiʃən]

29 obtain a sightseeing visa
[əbtéin]

30 foster more tourism
[túərìzm]

点数チェック

/10 /10 /10 /10 /10 /10 /10 /10 /10 /10

Unit 1-4

報道・マスメディア(1)

左の欄から言葉を選んで……を完成しよう！

31 人生相談欄担当のフリーライター
a fr……e advice co……st

32 信頼できる筋からの情報
information from a re……e s…ce

33 （マスコミに）新製品の発表をする
dis……e a press re……e

34 （野球などの）実況放送
a play-by-play co……ry

advertisement
campaign
columnist
commentary
correspondent
distribute
edition
freelance
issue
promotional
release
reliable
revenue
source
subscribe

35 雑誌を購読する
su……e to a magazine

36 戦場に特派員を派遣する
dispatch a co………nt to a war zone

37 12月号に掲載されている
published in the December i…e

38 朝刊に出る
appear in the morning e……n

39 新聞の広告収入
ad………nt re……e from the newspaper

40 販売促進運動を始める
kick off a pr……al ca…gn

一回で満点を取るより，何回もやってようやく満点を取る人の方が最後は勝つんだよ。
その方が頭の中の memory mechanism（記憶装置）にしっかり残るからだ。

Unit 1-4

フレーズ 31 個目から 40 個目までの答えをチェックしよう！　CD 5

31 a freelance advice columnist [kάləmnist]

32 information from a reliable source [riláiəbl]

33 distribute a press release [distríbjət]

34 a play-by-play commentary [kάməntèri]

35 subscribe to a magazine [səbskráib]

36 dispatch a correspondent to a war zone [kɔ̀:rəspάndənt]

37 published in the December issue [íʃu:]

38 appear in the morning edition [əpíə(r)]

39 advertisement revenue from the newspaper [révən(j)ù:]

40 kick off a promotional campaign [kæmpéin]

点数チェック
/10 /10 /10 /10 /10 /10 /10 /10 /10 /10

Unit 1-5

就職・キャリア (1)

左の欄から言葉を選んで……を完成しよう！

41	就職説明会に行く
	at...d a job f..r

42	職務内容の説明を読む
	check the job de........n

43	ネット上での求人掲示板
	on...e job bo..d

44	責任感ある几帳面(きちょうめん)な人を求めます
	a res......le and or......d person wanted

45	6ヶ月の試用期間
	a six-month pr......n pe...d

46	雇用（人員）削減
	a job cu....k

47	人材開発部
	human re......s and de........t department

48	給料をもらう
	get a pa.....k

49	履歴書を電子メールで提出して下さい。
	Su...t your résumé on...e.

50	採用条件
	a hiring po...y

attend
board
cutback
description
development
fair
online
organized
paycheck
period
policy
probation
resources
responsible
submit

一回で満点を取るより，何回もやってようやく満点を取る人の方が最後は勝つんだよ。その方が頭の中のmemory mechanism（記憶装置）にしっかり残るからだ。

Unit 1-5

フレーズ 41 個目から 50 個目までの答えをチェックしよう！ CD 6

41 **attend a job fair**
[əténd]

42 **check the job description**
[diskrípʃən]

43 **online job board**
[bɔ́:rd]

44 **a responsible and organized person wanted**
[rispánsəbl]   [ɔ́:rgənàizd]

45 **a six-month probation* period**
[proubéiʃən] *同義語 **trial period**

46 **a job cutback**
[kʌ́tbæk]

47 **human resources and development department**
[rí:sɔ:rsiz]   [divéləpmənt]

48 **get a paycheck**
[peitʃék]

49 **Submit your résumé online.**
[səbmít]   [rézəmèi]

50 **a hiring policy**
[páləsi]

点数チェック
/10 /10 /10 /10 /10 /10 /10 /10 /10 /10

Review Quiz for Unit 1

ではここまで演習してきたら、君の記憶はかんぺきなはず。そこで Unit のおさらいをしよう。テキストを見ずに文の .... を埋められるかな？ 何度でも復習できるように、書き込みはせずにやってみよう。

ここにある文は、実際の「TOIEC Part 5 短文穴埋め問題」のものとほぼ同じ長さになっている。だからこの REVIEW QUIZ も TOEIC と同じペースで、1問を15秒以内で答えるようにしよう。

1回目は絶対に辞書を使わないこと！キーワードを拾って記憶で勝負！

必要に応じて、語形を変えることを忘れないように。
タイマーを5分に設定して、READY SET GO！　　　　　CD 7

1. All soccer players have to stay .... to keep up with the hard work of constantly running up and down the pitch.

2. The forest fire in California was finally put out thanks to the efforts of ....

3. Did you watch the Marching Band contest last night? Did you see all those .... ?

4. You really have to be careful when you talk to .... like Daphne.

5. Bernie made .... for his mistake, but it didn't work this time and he got fired.

6. One of these days, I'm going to .... with Jud. I got beaten up twice already.

7. I was nervous about my new job, but the office has a really .... , so I feel very comfortable there already.

8. Nelly is having .... about marriage. She is beginning to think she is too young to get married.

9. We have .... so that you will be able to stay in Munich for one more day and enjoy the Beer Festival.

10. We hope that the opening of the new art center will .... in this city.

11. .... for this flight is New York with a stopover in Detroit.

12. A: Oh, no! I think I left my mobile phone on the train.
    B: Don't panic! Let's go ask at ....

13. The company's .... begins today. So get out there and sell our new products!

14. After writing for the *New York Times* for 10 years, Meg decided to become ....

15. Information from .... says there will be a reshuffling of the project members within the next week.

16. Did you know that a high percentage of media income comes from .... ?

17. Our .... department will start recruiting new college graduates in July.

18. Be sure to check .... before you decide to apply for the position.

19. Please .... by March 11th so that it reaches us before we start interviewing on March 20th.

Review Quiz for Unit 1

20. You will formally become a full-time worker and be given company business cards after completing the three-month ....

1. **Answer** lean and agile
   ピッチを絶えず行ったり来たり走り回るというハードな運動を維持するため，サッカー選手たちは皆ひき締まって機敏な身体つきをしている。

2. **Answer** courageous and devoted firefighters
   カリフォルニアの森林火災は勇敢で大胆な消防士たちの懸命な努力のおかげで消火した。

3. **Answer** splendid pageant participants
   ゆうべのマーチングバンドコンテストを見たかい？ 素晴らしいペイジェントの参加者たちを見たかい？

4. **Answer** a sensitive teenager
   ダフネのような感じやすいティーンエイジャーに話すときは気を付けなきゃいかんよ。

5. **Answer** a feeble excuse
   バーニーは自分のミスのことでいい加減な言い訳をしたが，今回はうまくいかず，彼はくびになった。

6. **Answer** get even
   近いうちきっと，ジャッドに仕返ししてやる。もう2度もひどくなぐられたんだ。

7. **Answer** hospitable atmosphere
   新しい仕事で心配だったけど，オフィスはとても暖かい雰囲気で，快適だ。

8. **Answer** second thoughts
   ネリーは結婚について考えが変わってきている。まだ結婚には若すぎると思い始めたのだ。

9. **Answer** arranged your itinerary
   ミュンヘンではもう一日滞在してビール祭りをお楽しみになれるよう旅程表を作成しました。

10. **Answer** foster more tourism
　　新しい美術センターの開館が市の観光業を促進することを願う。

11. **Answer** The final port of destination
　　この機はデトロイトに寄港し最終到着地はニューヨークです。

12. **Answer** the lost-and-found window
　　A: 携帯電話を電車に忘れてきたよ。
　　B: 慌てないで！ 遺失物取扱所に聞いてみると良いよ。

13. **Answer** promotional campaign
　　本日よりわが社の販売促進運動を始める。皆総出で新製品を売りまくろう！

14. **Answer** a freelance columnist
　　ニューヨークタイムズで10年執筆したのち，メグはフリーの寄稿者になることにした。

15. **Answer** a reliable source
　　信頼すべき筋からの情報によれば，来週中にプロジェクトメンバーの入れ替えがあるそうだ。

16. **Answer** advertising revenue
　　メディア業界の収入源の多くは広告収入だって知ってました？

17. **Answer** human resources and development
　　人材開発部は大学新卒の採用を7月から始める。

18. **Answer** the job description
　　その仕事に申し込む前に必ず職務内容をチェックすること。

19. **Answer** submit your résumé
　　3月20日の面接に間に合うよう3月11日までに履歴書を提出して下さい。

20. **Answer** probation period
　　仮採用期間が終了したら，正式社員になり，社名入りの名刺を持つことができる。

Power Builder Chart

/20	/20	/20	/20	/20	/20	/20	/20	/20	/20

黒猫トントンのちょっとブレイク 1

People and the Characters
猫はいろいろ，人もいろいろ

このエッセイに出てくる黒猫トントンは **delinquent tomcat** 不良オス猫だけど，それなりに **trying to work his way up** なんとか向上しようとしているんだ。だから，オーガも **abandon him to live as a stray cat** 彼を見捨ててのら猫にする勇気がないんだ。

だが，**how Ton Ton sees himself**「トントンが考えている自分」と **how Ooga sees Ton Ton**「オーガが観察するトントンの性格」とはかなり違うみたいだ。**Actually, they are quite the opposite of each other.** それどころか，どうも正反対の印象を持っているといってもよい。

反対同士結べるかな？

Quiz 1

Ton Ton thinks he is always:
1. gentle and sensitive
2. modest and unselfish
3. withdrawn and quiet
4. thrifty and humble
5. careful and discreet
6. hardworking and efficient
7. intelligent and thoughtful
8. hospitable and polite

Ooga thinks Ton Ton is:
a. careless and indiscreet
b. lazy and inefficient
c. rude and boisterous
d. rough and insensitive
e. wasteful and extravagant
f. foolish and thoughtless
g. bold and demanding
h. outgoing and noisy

On the other hand, this is how Ooga evaluates herself.
かたや，オーガは自分のことをこのように評価している。
Ton Ton got knocked out! トントンは，ビックリ仰天ひっくり返っちまった！

Quiz 2

Ooga thinks she is always:
1. caring and generous
2. clear and concise
3. thoughtful and logical
4. up-to-date and refined
5. punctual and knowledgeable
6. extroverted and sociable
7. flexible and eloquent
8. friendly and lovable

Ton Ton thinks Ooga is:
a. inconsiderate and illogical
b. tardy and ignorant
c. self-centered and stingy
d. abrasive and mean
e. vague and inarticulate
f. old-fashioned and crude
g. introverted and unsociable
h. stubborn and taciturn

Quiz 1

正解と訳

1. 優しく繊細な ― d. 乱暴で無分別
2. 謙虚で遠慮深い ― g. 出しゃばりで図々しい
3. 内気でおとなしい ― h. 外向的で騒々しい
4. 倹約でつつましい ― e. 浪費的でぜいたく
5. 注意深く分別がある ― a. 注意散漫で無分別
6. 働き者で有能 ― b. 怠け者で無能
7. 知的で思いやりがある ― f. アホで思いやりがない
8. 親切で礼儀正しい ― c. 無礼で荒っぽい

Quiz 2

正解と訳

1. 面倒見よく，寛容 ― c. 自己中心的でけちんぼ
2. 明晰(めいせき)で正確 ― e. はっきりせず口下手
3. 思慮深く論理的 ― a. 無分別で非論理的
4. 先進的で洗練されている ― f. 時代遅れでダサイ
5. 規則正しく，知識豊富 ― b. 遅刻するし無知
6. 外向性で社交的 ― g. 内向的で非社交的
7. 柔軟性があって雄弁 ― h. 頑固で無口
8. 親しみやすく愛すべき性格 ― d. 角の立つ性格で意地悪

28

Unit 2-1

人の性格・容姿（2）

左の欄から言葉を選んで……を完成しよう！

adventurous
advisor
amiable
competent
considerate
coworkers
entertaining
inefficient
inquisitive
masculine
skeptical
superintendent
teller
tempered

51 有能な同僚たち
com.....t co.....rs

52 愛想良い銀行の窓口係
an am....e bank te...r

53 役に立たずの管理人
an in........t su..........nt

54 芸達者なサーカスの道化師たち
en........g circus clowns

55 筋肉もりもりカンフーの達人
a ma......e kung fu master

56 思いやりある担任の先生
a co.......te class ad....r

57 すべてに疑い深い
sk......l about everything

58 短気なボス
short-te....ed chief

59 詮索好きな隣人
an in.......ve neighbor

60 冒険好きで向こう見ずな若者
an ad........s and bold young man

一回で満点を取るより，何回もやってようやく満点を取る人の方が最後は勝つんだよ。
その方が頭の中の memory mechanism（記憶装置）にしっかり残るからだ。

Unit 2-1

フレーズ 51 個目から 60 個目までの答えをチェックしよう！　CD 8

51 **competent coworkers**
[kámpətnt]

52 **an amiable bank teller**
[éimiəbl]

53 **an inefficient superintendent**
[ìnifíʃnt]

54 **entertaining circus clowns**
[èntə(r)téiniŋ]

55 **a masculine kung fu master**
[mǽskjələn]

56 **a considerate* class advisor**
[kənsídərət] *considerable …「大量の」「注目すべき」との違いに注意

57 **skeptical about everything**
[sképtikəl]

58 **short-tempered chief**
[témpərd]

59 **an inquisitive neighbor**
[inkwízətiv]

60 **an adventurous and bold young man**
[ædvéntʃərəs]

点数チェック

/10 /10 /10 /10 /10 /10 /10 /10 /10 /10

Unit 2-2

ボランティア活動

左の欄から言葉を選んで......を完成しよう！

61 無償で通訳として働く
work as an in........r on a pro bono basis

62 慈善活動をする
work for ch......le c...es

63 ホームレスのため給食活動をする
run a s..p ki....n for homeless people

64 命綱の緊急食料を配る
supply re...f food as a li.....e

65 危機管理センターを設営する
set up a cr...s center

66 非営利組織（NPO）の活動を支援する
support the ac......es of a nonprofit or.........n (NPO)

67 心の問題のカウンセリングをする
counseling for em.....al problems

68 津波被害者のために寄付金を募る
take up a co.......n for tsunami vi...ms

69 戦争避難民のため避難所を設営する
set up a shelter for war re....es

70 基金集めのためのイベントを企画する
plan a fu......er event

activities
causes
charitable
collection
crisis
emotional
fundraiser
interpreter
kitchen
lifeline
organization
refugees
relief
soup
victims

一回で満点を取るより，何回もやってようやく満点を取る人の方が最後は勝つんだよ。
その方が頭の中の memory mechanism（記憶装置）にしっかり残るからだ。

Unit 2-2

フレーズ61個目から70個目までの答えをチェックしよう！　CD 9

61 work as an interpreter on a pro bono basis
[intə́:rpritər] [prou-bóunou]

62 work for charitable causes
[tʃǽrətəbl]

63 run a soup kitchen for homeless people
[sú:p] [kítʃən]

64 supply relief food as a lifeline
[rilí:f]

65 set up a crisis center
[kráisis]

66 support the activities of a nonprofit organization (NPO)
[ɔ̀:rgənizéiʃən]

67 counseling for emotional problems
[imóuʃənl]

68 take up a collection for tsunami victims
[víktimz]

69 set up a shelter for war refugees
[rèfjudʒí:z]

70 plan a fundraiser event
[fʌ́ndrèizər]

点数チェック
/10 /10 /10 /10 /10 /10 /10 /10 /10 /10

Unit 2-3

車・ドライブ

左の欄から言葉を選んで……を完成しよう！

71	数珠(じゅず)つなぎの渋滞
	bumper-to-bumper tr....c

72	エンストしたトラックを牽引(けんいん)する
	tow the st...ed truck

73	回数券を買って電車代を節約しよう。
	Buy co...n tickets and save on the train f..e.

74	飲酒または麻薬の影響下の運転
	dr...ng under the in......e

assistance
breakdown
coupon
crosswalk
driving
expired
fare
feed
influence
learner's
pedestrian
permit
reckless
stalled
traffic

75	牽引車サービスを呼ぶ
	call for roadside as.......e

76	歩行者用横断路
	a pe......an cr......k

77	乱暴な運転
	re.....s dr...ng

78	時間切れの駐車メーターに料金を入れる
	f..d the ex....d parking meter

79	仮免許証を取る
	get a le....r's pe...t

80	（緊急車両用の）路肩(ろかた)車線に入るな。
	Stay out of the br......n lane.

一回で満点を取るより，何回もやってようやく満点を取る人の方が最後は勝つんだよ。その方が頭の中の memory mechanism（記憶装置）にしっかり残るからだ。

Unit 2-3

フレーズ 71 個目から 80 個目までの答えをチェックしよう！　CD10

71 **bumper-to-bumper traffic**
[bʌ́mpər]

72 **tow the stalled truck**
[tóu]　　　[stɔ́:ld]

73 **Buy coupon tickets and save on the train fare.**
[kú:pɑn]

74 **driving under the influence**
[ínfluəns] *DUI と短縮される。

75 **call for roadside assistance**
[əsístəns]

76 **a pedestrian crosswalk**
[pədéstriən]

77 **reckless driving**
[rékləs]

78 **feed the expired parking meter**
[ikspáiərd]

79 **get a learner's permit**
[pə́rmit]

80 **Stay out of the breakdown lane.**
[bréik-dàun]

点数チェック

Unit 2-4

エコロジー

左の欄から言葉を選んで…… を完成しよう！

81 熱帯雨林の急速な消滅
rapid dis………e of the r..n forest

82 大気と水質汚染
air and water po……n

83 環境問題を意識する
become aware of ec…….l problems

84 原子炉の融解
a me…..n at the nu….r reactor

caution
combustible
disappearance
ecological
extinct
global
green
meltdown
nuclear
pollution
rain
resources
site
sustainable
warming

85 注意！ カドミューム（汚染）地域
Ca….n! Cadmium s..e.

86 環境問題コーディネーター
a g…n coordinator

87 絶滅する
become ex….t

88 可燃ゴミ
com……le trash

89 地球温暖化
gl…l wa….g

90 天然資源の持続的な利用
su…….le use of natural re……s

一回で満点を取るより，何回もやってようやく満点を取る人の方が最後は勝つんだよ。その方が頭の中の memory mechanism（記憶装置）にしっかり残るからだ。

Unit 2-4

フレーズ 81 個目から 90 個目までの答えをチェックしよう！ CD11

81 rapid disappearance of the rain forest
[dìsəpíərəns]

82 air and water pollution
[pəlúːʃən]

83 become aware of ecological problems
[èkəládʒikəl]

84 a meltdown at the nuclear reactor
[njúːkliər]

85 Caution! Cadmium site.
[kædmiəm]

86 a green coordinator
[kouɔ́ːrdənèitər]

87 become extinct
[ikstíŋkt]

88 combustible trash
[kəmbʌ́stəbl]

89 global warming
[glóubəl]

90 sustainable use of natural resources
[səstéinəbl]

点数チェック

Unit 2-5

ビジネス・基礎編 (1)

左の欄から言葉を選んで…… を完成しよう！

91	前もって通知する
	no...y in ad....e

92	ややこしい手続きを踏む
	go through red t..e

93	プロジェクトの承認を得た
	got an ap.....l of the project

94	見込み客に接近する
	ap.....h po.....al clients

95	建設的なアドバイスをする
	offer co........ve advice

advance
amalgamation
approach
approval
constructive
estimate
fill
notify
potential
proficient
purchase
rival
tape
urgent

96	ロシア語に堪能(たんのう)
	pr.......t in Russian

97	競争企業同士の合併
	am.........n of two ri..l firms

98	見積額は金曜日までに必要
	es.....e figures requested by Friday

99	買い注文をキャンセルする
	cancel the pu.....e order

100	急ぎの注文に応じる
	f..l an ur...t order

一回で満点を取るより, 何回もやってようやく満点を取る人の方が最後は勝つんだよ。その方が頭の中の memory mechanism (記憶装置) にしっかり残るからだ。

Unit 2-5

フレーズ 91 個目から 100 個目までの答えをチェックしよう！　CD12

91 **notify in advance**
[nóutəfài]　[ædvǽns]

92 **go through red tape**

93 **got an approval of the project**
[əprúːvəl]

94 **approach potential clients**
[pəténʃəl]　[kláiənts]

95 **offer constructive advice**
[kənstrʌ́ktiv]

96 **proficient in Russian**
[prəfíʃənt]

97 **amalgamation of two rival firms**
[əmælgəméiʃən]

98 **estimate figures requested by Friday**
[éstəmət]

99 **cancel the purchase order**
[pə́ːrtʃəs]

100 **fill an urgent order**
[ə́ːrdʒənt]

点数チェック

/10 /10 /10 /10 /10 /10 /10 /10 /10

Review Quiz for Unit 2 ▎39

ではここまで演習してきたら，君の記憶はかんぺきなはず。そこで Unit のおさらいをしよう。テキストを見ずに文の .... を埋められるかな？何度でも復習できるように，書き込みはせずにやってみよう。

ここにある文は，実際の「TOIEC Part 5 短文穴埋め問題」のものとほぼ同じ長さになっている。だからこの REVIEW QUIZ も TOEIC と同じペースで，1問を 15 秒以内で答えるようにしよう。

1回目は絶対に辞書を使わないこと！キーワードを拾って記憶で勝負！

必要に応じて，語形を変えることを忘れないように。
タイマーを5分に設定して，READY SET GO！ CD13

1. Thanks to our highly .... , we were the first company to develop a new drug for the flu.

2. The air conditioning system in our apartment building is never going to be fixed properly as long as we have such ....

3. Henry had .... who really helped him a lot. Otherwise, he may not have been able to graduate this spring.

4. The only problem with my new apartment is that I have .... who watches everything.

5. Barney had done lots of volunteer work for various .... at the hospital before he became a registered nurse.

6. All of the money earned at the weekend bazaar will be sent to .... for abused women.

7. The region's population is growing rapidly because so many .... fled there from the neighboring country.

8. Jeff's house burned down, so his friends are planning to .... to help him out.

9. Oh, no! We won't be able to get off the expressway until they remove .... on the exit ramp.

10. Stan will surely lose his license if he gets caught .... again.

11. The accident wasn't my fault; I was crossing in ....

12. .... drove onto the sidewalk, hitting several pedestrians.

13. The Japanese crested ibis (toki) .... in 2003.

14. The workers worked for 48 hours straight to keep .... from melting down.

15. In my city, we are requested to separate .... from others such as glass and plastics.

16. The president's proposal calls for .... of the nation's water and soil resources.

17. Our newly redecorated showroom will make it easier for .... to see our entire product line.

18. If you want to advance in this business, it is important to be .... English and computers.

19. Why are the shipping costs running over .... our transporters originally gave us?

20. Can someone please tell me what happened to .... for 10 office chairs we placed two weeks ago?

Review Quiz for Unit 2 🔊41

1. **Answer** competent coworkers
   有能な同僚たちのおかげで,我が社は一番にインフルエンザ用の新薬を製造できた。

2. **Answer** an inefficient superintendent
   あんな無能な管理人がいる限り,家のアパートビルのエアコンシステムは絶対ちゃんとなおらないさ。

3. **Answer** a considerate advisor
   ヘンリーは思いやりある担任からすごく助けてもらえた。でなければ,彼は今年の春卒業できなかっただろうね。

4. **Answer** an inquisitive neighbor
   新しいアパートで一つ困るのは,詮索好きの隣人がいて,いつも見ていることだ。

5. **Answer** charitable causes
   バーニーは正看護師になる前は,病院で色々な奉仕活動をした。

6. **Answer** a crisis center
   週末バザーからの収益金は全て,虐待を受けた女性のための救援センターに寄付される。

7. **Answer** war refugees
   隣国からの多数の戦争避難民が移入してきているので,この地域の人口は急速に増加している。

8. **Answer** take up a collection
   ジェフの家は火事で焼かれてしまったので,友人たちは彼のために募金しようとしている。

9. **Answer** the stalled truck
   困るなあ! あの高速出口でエンストしたトラックを移動しなければ,高速から降りられないよ。

10. **Answer** driving under the influence
    もう一度飲酒運転で捕まれば,スタンは確実に免許を取り上げられる。

11. **Answer** the pedestrian crosswalk
    事故は私の落ち度じゃない；私は歩行者横断道路を渡っていたのだから。

12. **Answer** A reckless driver
    無謀運転手は歩道に乗り上げ，数人の歩行者をはねた。

13. **Answer** became extinct
    日本トキは 2003 年に絶滅した。

14. **Answer** the nuclear reactor
    作業員たちは，原子炉の臨界事故を防ぐため，不眠不休で 48 時間働いた。

15. **Answer** the combustible trash
    わが市では，可燃ゴミはガラス類やプラスチックなどの不燃ゴミから分別することになっています。

16. **Answer** the sustainable use
    大統領は国内の水，土壌資源の継続的な使用ができる環境を提案している。

17. **Answer** potential clients
    新しく改装されたショールームは，見込み客たちにとって，我が社すべての製品ラインがより理解しやすくなっている。

18. **Answer** proficient in
    この業界で出世したいならば，英語とコンピューターに長けていることが肝要だ。

19. **Answer** the estimated figures
    運送代が，運送会社が始めに提出した見積額より多くなっているのは何故ですか。

20. **Answer** the urgent order
    2 週間前に出した，オフィス用椅子 10 脚の急ぎ注文はいったいどうなったのか，誰か分かるかな？

Power Builder Chart

| /20 | /20 | /20 | /20 | /20 | /20 | /20 | /20 | /20 | /20 |

黒猫トントンのちょっとブレイク 2

I Was Shocked by Your Shocking Words!
君のショッキングな言葉はショックだー！

オーガ： オーイ，トントン。ちょっと来なさい。英語で，"Do you have any interest in mole hunting?"「モグラ狩りに興味ある?」と聞かれたら君はなんと応えるかな。

トントン： エー, そんなの簡単じゃん。
Yes, I'm very interesting!

オーガ： ブー！ それじゃ「私は面白い人です。」という意味になっちまうぞ。では今日は interesting と interested との違いについて説明するから，良く覚えて，そういう embarrassing mistake 恥ずかしい間違いをしないように，気を付けなさい。

トントン： へーい。(There goes my chance to go on a mole hunting date with Bun Bun. Darn! せっかく, 雌猫ブンブンをモグラ狩りに誘うチャンスだったのになあ。ちぇっ!)

ちょっと考えなければどっちが正しいか答えが出ない人は，結構 non-native speakers of English 英語のネイティブでない人には多いよね。
上の会話中の文の意味はこうだ。

1) "Yes, I'm very interesting." は『私はとても面白い人よ。』
2) "Yes, I'm very interested." は『とても興味がある。』

一応, -ing は通常，物・事に付く表現または人の性格表現。-ed は人に付く感情表現と覚えよう。

これを間違えるのは，黒猫トントンだけではないよ。私の友人で，20 年以上もロスに暮らしたハチローも，私が, "Do you have any interest in going to see the new movie 'Cloning'?" と誘うと彼は "I'm very interesting." と答える。で，そのたびに私は, have to stifle a laugh

笑いをかみ殺すのに苦労するんだ。きっと誰も直してくれないままずっと暮らしてきたのだろう。何しろロスというのは，**multiethnic and multicultural society** 多民族からなる多文化社会だから，いちいち相手の言ったことを直さないで，そのまま折り合って暮らしていることが多い。いっぱしのビジネスマンのハチローに私がいまさら指摘するのもなあ，なにかはばかられるしー。

かくいうオーガも，しつこくしつこく練習して，ようやく native の感覚が身についたの。それまでは，やっぱり，随分恥をかいたものさ。一番お勧めするのは，いくつかの例文を暗記しておくこと。君たちも，**persistently and repetitiously** しつこく繰り返し練習して欲しい。まず次の文で良いと思われる文に○を付けてみよう。

☐ 1a. It was such a fascinated painting that I just stood there staring at it.
☐ 1b. It was such a fascinating painting that I just stood there staring at it.

☐ 2a. I'm boring. Let's get out of here.
☐ 2b. I'm bored. Let's get out of here.

☐ 3a. I'm so discouraged by the test results.
☐ 3b. I'm so discouraging by the test results.

☐ 4a. You're so amused. You should become a comedian.
☐ 4b. You're so amusing. You should become a comedian.

☐ 5a. I'm so excited. I'm going to be in a Brad Pitt movie!
☐ 5b. I'm so exciting. I'm going to be in Brad Pitt movie!

☐ 6a. The noise was really loud and annoyed, so I complained.
☐ 6b. The noise was really loud and annoying, so I complained.

☐ 7a. It's really confused. Try to explain more clearly.
☐ 7b. It's really confusing. Try to explain more clearly.

Touchy Points

常識的には，君は I'm interested, bored, amazed, tired, satisfied, stunned, などとは言っても良いが, I'm interesting, amazing, satisfying, stunning などとは言わない方が良いと思うよ。相手はきっと君のことを very conceited person 自惚れ屋と思うだろうからね。

正解と訳

1. b：その絵があまりに素晴らしいので，じっと見入って動けなかった。
2. b：もう退屈したから，出ようよ。
3. a：テストの成績にがっかりした。
4. b：君はすごく面白いね。コメディアンになるといいよ。
5. a：すっごくうれしい。今度ブラッド・ピットの映画に出るんだぜー。
6. b：すごい大きな音がした。私は頭に来て，文句を言った。
7. a：訳が分からないよ。もっときちんと説明してよ。

46

Unit 3-1

人の性格・容姿 (3)

左の欄から言葉を選んで……を完成しよう！

101 やる気満々の野心家
a highly mo……d go-getter

102 鑑賞力のある観客
an ap……ve audience

103 頑強でどっしりタイプのログビルダー
a ro…t and st…y log builder

104 腰の曲がった高齢者
a st…ed-over elderly person

105 おおらかで陽気なバーテンダー
an ea……g and ch…..l bartender

106 社交的なパーティの主人
a so….le party host

107 気難しい客
a hard-to-pl…e cl…t

108 決断力を持った先駆者
a de……ed fr……..r

109 キャリア組と専業主婦・主夫
a career person and a ho……r

110 料理が趣味の人
a cooking en…….t

appreciative
cheerful
client
determined
easygoing
enthusiast
frontrunner
homemaker
motivated
please
robust
sociable
stocky
stooped

一回で満点を取るより, 何回もやってようやく満点を取る人の方が最後は勝つんだよ。その方が頭の中の memory mechanism（記憶装置）にしっかり残るからだ。

Unit 3-1

フレーズ 101 個目から 110 個目までの答えをチェックしよう！　CD14

101 **a highly motivated go-getter**
[móutəvèitid]

102 **an appreciative audience**
[əprí:ʃətiv]

103 **a robust and stocky log builder**
[roubʌ́st]　　　[stʌ́ki]

104 **a stooped-over elderly person**
[stú:pt]

105 **an easygoing and cheerful bartender**
[tʃíərfəl]

106 **a sociable party host**
[sóuʃəbl]

107 **a hard-to-please client**
[kláiənt]

108 **a determined frontrunner**
[ditə́:rmind]　　[frʌ́nt-rʌ̀nər]

109 **a career person and a homemaker**
[kəríər]

110 **a cooking enthusiast**
[inθú:ziæst]

点数チェック

/10 /10 /10 /10 /10 /10 /10 /10 /10 /10

Unit 3-2

旅行・ホテル

左の欄から言葉を選んで……を完成しよう！

111 海側の部屋を予約する
b..k a room with an ocean v..w

112 長期滞在レートはご相談に応じます
willing to ne……e for long-stay rates

113 （ホテルなど）無料提供のリフレッシュ用品
co………ry am……es

114 豪華な続き部屋
a lu……s su..e

accommodations
amenities
book
cancellation
catering
complimentary
concierge
hike
hospitality
luxurious
minute
negotiate
particular
suite
view

115 サービス業界で働く
work in the ho……ty industry

116 直前の取消し；ドタキャン
last-mi...e ca………n

117 コンシェルジェは客の特別な要望に応える。
A con…..e meets the customer's pa……r requests.

118 シーズン最盛期の料金値上げ
peak season price h..e

119 自炊用ホステル
a self-ca…..g hostel

120 ホテル宿泊の手配をする
arrange hotel ac………ns

一回で満点を取るより，何回もやってようやく満点を取る人の方が最後は勝つんだよ。その方が頭の中の memory mechanism（記憶装置）にしっかり残るからだ。

Unit 3-2

フレーズ111個目から120個目までの答えをチェックしよう！ CD15

111 book a room with an ocean view
[óuʃən]

112 willing to negotiate for long-stay rates
[nigóuʃièit]

113 complimentary amenities
[kàmpləméntəri]

114 a luxurious suite
[lʌgʒúəriəs] [swíːt]

115 work in the hospitality industry
[hàspətǽləti]

116 last-minute cancellation
[kænsəléiʃən]

117 A concierge meets the customer's particular requests.
[pərtíkjulər]

118 peak season price hike
[háik]

119 a self-catering hostel
[kéitəriŋ]

120 arrange hotel accommodations
[əkàmədéiʃən]

点数チェック

/10 /10 /10 /10 /10 /10 /10 /10 /10 /10

Unit 3-3

就職・キャリア(2)

左の欄から言葉を選んで......を完成しよう！

121 適格な採用候補者
a su.....e ca.....te for the position

122 一律に5％の昇給
a 5% raise across the bo..d

123 新入社員向け研修会
a new em.....e or........n workshop

124 平均月収
av....e monthly in...e

accept
average
board
candidate
employee
income
offer
orientation
overtime
professional
references
starting
suitable
training
workweek

125 初任給を決める
discuss a st.....g salary

126 残業をする
work ov.....e

127 採用内定を承諾する
ac...t a job of..r

128 実習期間
on-the-job tr.....g period

129 現職の推薦者3名を要す
three pr........al re......es required

130 週5日勤務制
a five-day w......k

一回で満点を取るより，何回もやってようやく満点を取る人の方が最後は勝つんだよ。その方が頭の中のmemory mechanism（記憶装置）にしっかり残るからだ。

Unit 3-3

フレーズ 121 個目から 130 個目までの答えをチェックしよう！　CD16

121 a suitable candidate for the position
[kǽndidət]

122 a 5% raise across the board
[réiz]

123 a new employee orientation workshop
[èmplɔ́iː]

124 average monthly income
[ǽvəridʒ]

125 discuss a starting salary
[sǽləri]

126 work overtime*
　　*overworked「働き過ぎ」と間違えないように.

127 accept a job offer
[æksépt]

128 on-the-job training period
[píəriəd]

129 three professional references required*
[réfərənsiz]
*欧米で再就職の際は,同じ専門分野での推薦人または身元保証人3名が必要な場合が多い.

130 a five-day workweek
[wə́ːrk-wiːk]

点数チェック

| /10 | /10 | /10 | /10 | /10 | /10 | /10 | /10 | /10 |

Unit 3-4

健康と病気（1）

左の欄から言葉を選んで……を完成しよう！

131 保健所
a he……e center

132 102°Fの熱がある
run a te……..e of 102°F

133 喫煙は心不全になるリスクを2倍にする。
Smoking doubles the r..k of heart fa….e.

134 偏頭痛がする
have a migraine he…..e

135 悪性腫瘍
a ma……t tumor

136 杉花粉アレルギー
a cedar po…n allergy

137 健康診断を受ける
get a ph…..l checkup

138 歯科の予約を延ばす
po…..e a de…l appointment

139 発疹を掻いては駄目！
Don't sc….h the r..h!

140 医師の処方箋をもって薬局で薬を買う
have a pr………n fi…d at the pharmacy

dental
failure
filled
headache
healthcare
malignant
physical
pollen
postpone
prescription
rash
risk
scratch
temperature

一回で満点を取るより、何回もやってようやく満点を取る人の方が最後は勝つんだよ。
その方が頭の中のmemory mechanism（記憶装置）にしっかり残るからだ。

Unit 3-4

フレーズ 131 個目から 140 個目までの答えをチェックしよう！　CD17

131 a healthcare center
[hélθ-kèər]

132 run a temperature of 102°F*
[témpərtʃùər] *Fahrenheit　102°F は約 40°C

133 Smoking doubles the risk of heart failure.
[féiljər]

134 have a migraine headache
[máigrein]　[hédèik]

135 a malignant tumor
[məlígnənt]　[tjúːmər] *nonmalignant tumor ... 良性腫瘍

136 a cedar pollen allergy
[pálən]　[ǽlərdʒi]

137 get a physical checkup
[fízikəl]

138 postpone* a dental appointment
[pous(t)póun] *発音注意。「ポスポーン」't' は発音しない。

139 Don't scratch the rash!
[skrætʃ]

140 have a prescription filled at the pharmacy
[priskrípʃən]

点数チェック

Unit 3-5

ビジネス・基礎編(2)

左の欄から言葉を選んで......を完成しよう！

141 社用の文房具
company st......y su....es

142 請求書を送る
send an in....e

143 高騰する燃料価格
sk........g f..l prices

144 新企画に任ぜられる
as.....d to the new project

145 共同経営者
a business as......e

146 支店へ転勤になる
be tr.......ed to a branch office

147 諸経費として処理する
file as a mi..........s expense

148 現金問屋
cash-and-carry wh.......r

149 記録的な利益を得る
make a record pr...t

150 自分の連絡先を残す
leave one's co....t in........n

assigned
associate
contact
fuel
information
invoice
miscellaneous
profit
skyrocketing
stationery
supplies
transferred
wholesaler

一回で満点を取るより、何回もやってようやく満点を取る人の方が最後は勝つんだよ。その方が頭の中の memory mechanism (記憶装置) にしっかり残るからだ。

Unit 3-5

フレーズ 141 個目から 150 個目までの答えをチェックしよう！　CD18

141 **company stationery* supplies**
[stéiʃənèri] [səpláiz]
*意味注意。stationary …「静止状態；駐在」と間違えないように。

142 **send an invoice**
[ínvɔis]

143 **skyrocketing fuel prices**
[skàirákitíŋ] [fjúːəl]

144 **assigned to the new project**
[əsáind]

145 **a business associate**
[əsóuʃièit, -si-]

146 **be transferred* to a branch office**
[trænsfə́ːrd] *アクセント注意。動詞は「トランス**ファー**」、名詞は「**トランス**ファー」

147 **file as a miscellaneous expense**
[mìsəléiniəs]

148 **cash-and-carry wholesaler**
[hóulsélər]

149 **make a record* profit**
[rékɔːd] *アクセント注意。名詞は [rékɔːd] 動詞は [rikɔ́ːrd]

150 **leave one's contact information**
[kántækt]

点数チェック

/10 /10 /10 /10 /10 /10 /10 /10 /10 /10

Review Quiz for Unit 3

> ではここまで演習してきたら，君の記憶はかんぺきなはず。そこで Unit のおさらいをしよう。テキストを見ずに文の .... を埋められるかな？何度でも復習できるように，書き込みはせずにやってみよう。
>
> ここにある文は，実際の「TOIEC Part 5 短文穴埋め問題」のものとほぼ同じ長さになっている。だからこの REVIEW QUIZ も TOEIC と同じペースで，1問を 15 秒以内で答えるようにしよう。
>
> 1回目は絶対に辞書を使わないこと！キーワードを拾って記憶で勝負！
>
> 必要に応じて，語形を変えることを忘れないように。
> タイマーを5分に設定して，READY SET GO！　　CD19

1. We need someone aggressive in sales, so I think we should hire Ted Zemeckis who seems to be the most .... person of the five interviewees.

2. We had a really .... tonight. They always laughed at the right places in the play.

3. The opening reception was a great success thanks to our experienced and very ....

4. The new website features original recipes submitted by .... from all over the country.

5. If the other side is not .... on the price, we will have to find another supplier.

6. You don't need to pack toiletries. The hotel has all kinds of ....

7. Sharon enjoys working with people, so she is looking for a job in the ....

8. Our company takes pride in doing our best to satisfy any .... that our customers may have.

9. .... for the position should speak fluent English and have some experience in Asian trade markets.

10. Our target customers are families with .... of between $6,000 and $8,000.

11. I'm exhausted! I've had to .... almost every day this month.

12. We expect our employees to keep their skills up-to-date so we give them a lot of chances for ....

13. I think I am .... ! Feel my forehead. Is it hot?

14. The test showed that the young athlete had .... of the kidney.

15. You want to .... again? But your toothache isn't going to go away by itself. You really should go to see a dentist at once!

16. I have to stop by the pharmacy and .... It's a painkiller for my bad knee.

17. Anyone caught taking .... home from the office will be immediately let go. It's stealing!

18. Henry, I want you to meet .... of mine, Ted Booth. We've worked together since this company started.

19. If we want to keep the project within budget, we need to cut down on ....

Review Quiz for Unit 3 | 59

20. Please leave your .... with our receptionist at the end of the seminar so that we can keep you informed of future events.

1. **Answer** highly motivated
   わが社は販売に積極的な人材が必要だ。5名の面接者中一番やる気のあるように見えるテッド・ゼメキスを採用すべきだと思う。

2. **Answer** appreciative audience
   今夜は鑑賞力のある観客を得られて幸せだ。いつも勘所で笑ってくれたね。

3. **Answer** sociable party host
   開会式のレセプションは経験豊富で，とても社交に長けた主人役のおかげで，大成功だった。

4. **Answer** cooking enthusiasts
   新しいウエブサイトで，国中からの料理愛好家たちから募集した独創的な料理を特集しているよ。

5. **Answer** willing to negotiate
   相手方が値引き交渉に乗る意志がないのなら，違うサプライヤーをみつけなければならない。

6. **Answer** complimentary amenities
   洗面用具は荷物に入れなくて良いよ。ホテルには，いろいろな備え付けの衛生用品があるから。

7. **Answer** hospitality industry
   シャロンは人と交わって働くのが好きだから，接客サービス業の仕事を探している。

8. **Answer** particular requests
   私どもではお客様のいかなる特別なご要求があってもベストを尽くすことをしております。

9. **Answer** Suitable candidates
   この職種に申し込み資格があるのは，英語が流ちょうに話せて，アジア方面の貿易経験のある方です。

10. **Answer** an average monthly income
    わが社が狙う客筋は，月収6000ドルから8000ドルの家族です。

11. **Answer** work overtime
    もうくたくただよ。今月はほとんど毎日，残業だったんだから。

12. **Answer** on-the-job training
    わが社は社員たちに最新の技術を持ち続けることを期待します。故に，実習の機会を多く与えています。

13. **Answer** running a temperature
    熱があるみたい。額を触ってみてよ。熱いだろう？

14. **Answer** a malignant tumor
    検査の結果，その若い選手は腎臓に悪性腫瘍のあることが分かった。

15. **Answer** postpone your appointment
    また予約を延ばすって？ でも歯痛はひとりでに治ることはないんだよ。今すぐ，歯科に行きなさい！

16. **Answer** have my prescription filled
    薬局に寄って，薬を処方してもらわなくてはならない。膝の痛み止めなの。

17. **Answer** stationery supplies
    オフィスの事務用品を家に持ち帰るのを見つけたら，即解雇します。それは窃盗です！

18. **Answer** a business associate
    ヘンリー，私の共同経営者テッド・ブースをご紹介します。この会社を立ち上げたとき以来一緒に働いております。

19. **Answer** miscellaneous expenses
    このプロジェクトを予算以内に収めるには，諸経費を削らなければならない。

20. **Answer** contact information
    今後の催しなどについてご連絡できますように，このセミナーのあと，受付にあなた様のご連絡先をお残し下さい。

Power Builder Chart

/20	/20	/20	/20	/20	/20	/20	/20	/20	/20

黒猫トントンのちょっとブレイク 3

Polite Expressions
えっ！英語でも敬語ってあるの？

自由な国アメリカと思ったら大間違い！

トントン： 自由な国アメリカでは **hierarchy** 上下関係なんかナイナイ **polite expressions** 敬語なんて，ナイナイ。
ああ，ぼくも，オーガなんかにしごかれないで，早くアメリカに行って，**Yankee Doodle kitties** とつきあいたいよー。

黒猫トントンの思考力は狸以下ミミズ以上だとオーガがそばで怒っておる。ここでたまらず，トントンを押しのけてオーガ先生登場！
（"よーお，待ってました"でもないか。）

オーガ： **ignorant and rude** 無知で無礼なトントンのことは放っておいて，**polite and subtle expressions** について，私が一席。自由な国アメリカと思ったら大間違い。猫いるところ **hierarchy**（上下関係）あり。**hierarchy** あるところ敬語ありだ。とくにビジネス英語を多く出題する **TOEIC** では，この **subtle expressions** 微妙な言い回しを理解することはとても大切なんだ。

日本語では丁寧語「です，ます，ございます」，尊敬語「いらっしゃる，おっしゃる」謙譲語「申し上げる，伺う」などと語彙の違いがあるが，英語では，語彙の違いより言い回しの変化で相手への感情を表すことが多い。かなり回りくどい言い方になるほど，ていねい度が上がることになる。

例えば,「静かにしなさい。」などと相手に何かを要求するとき, **the least polite expression**,（一番直接的な表現）から **the most polite**（もっともていねいな順）にならべると

なにか要求するとき

ていねい度

Level
1. **Be quiet!**　静かにせい！
2. **Be quiet, please!**　静かにしなさい！
3. **Won't you be quiet, please?**　静かにしてくれない？
4. **Would you be quiet?**　静かにして下さいません？
5. **Would you mind being quiet?**
   静かにしていただけませんか？
6. **Could you please be quiet?**　静かにお願いできません？

Level
7. **I would really appreciate it if you could keep quite, please.**
   静かにして頂ければとてもありがたいんですけど。

相手の許可を得たいとき

ていねい度

Level
1. **Can I leave now?**　もう帰っても良いかい？
2. **May I leave now?**　もう帰っても良いですか？
3. **Could I leave now?**　もう失礼してよろしいでしょうか？

Level
4. **Would you mind if I left now?**
   もし宜しければ，失礼させて頂けますか？

黒猫トントンのちょっとブレイク 63

Touchy Points

許可を得るときの Can I ...? と May I ...? はその politeness ていねい度において, かなりの差がある。Can I は「～してもいいかなあ。」May I ...? は「～しても良いですか？」。そのときの状況にもよるが, 先生や, 上司に対して Can I ...? を使うと,「悪い印象を持たれる」または「注意される」ことがあるから気を付けよう。

64

Unit 4-1

人の感情と行動 (2)

左の欄から言葉を選んで …… を完成しよう！

151 率直にズバリと聞く
ask someone po..t bl..k

152 適切な判断を下す
make a so..d ju.....t

153 ヘンテコな行動
aw....d be.....r

154 患者の事が心配だ
feel co......d about a patient

155 適切な助言をする
give ap.......te advice

156 酒におぼれる
in....e in drinking

157 まともな考えをたたき込む
t..k se..e into someone

158 犬に怒鳴ったことを悔やむ
feel re......l about yelling at my dog

159 残念なミスだった。
It was a r........le mistake.

160 恨みをずっと忘れない
hold a gr...e against someone

appropriate
awkward
behavior
blank
concerned
grudge
indulge
judgment
point
regretful
regrettable
sense
sound
talk

一回で満点を取るより, 何回もやってようやく満点を取る人の方が最後は勝つんだよ。その方が頭の中のmemory mechanism（記憶装置）にしっかり残るからだ。

Unit 4-1

フレーズ 151 個目から 160 個目までの答えをチェックしよう！ CD20

151 ask someone point blank
[pɔ́int] [blǽŋk]

152 make a sound judgment
[dʒʌ́dʒmənt]

153 awkward behavior
[ɔ́:kwərd]

154 feel concerned about a patient
[kənsə́:rnd]

155 give appropriate advice
[əpróupriət]

156 indulge in drinking
[indʌ́ldʒ]

157 talk sense into someone
[séns]

158 feel regretful about yelling at my dog
[rigrétfəl] [jéliŋ]

159 It was a regrettable* mistake.
[rigrétəbl] *regretful「後悔する」は人の感情についていう。だから主語は人物。
regrettable「残念な事だ」は出来事についていう。だから主語は物事。

160 hold a grudge against someone
[grʌ́dʒ]

点数チェック

Unit 4-2

報道・マスメディア（2）

左の欄から言葉を選んで……を完成しよう！

161 編集長
e....r-in-ch..f

162 有名人本人に会う
meet a ce......y in pe...n

163 王室結婚式のニュースが見出しを独占。
Royal wedding news do......d the headlines.

164 著名な受賞作家
an em....t, aw..d-winning writer

165 宣伝ポスターを貼る
put up pu......y posters

166 インターネットを利用した報道活動
ele......c jo.......m

167 緊急速報のために番組を中断します。
We in......t this program for a special bu.....n.

168 広範囲なニュース取材
wide co.....e of the news

169 インターネットを使って参加するボランティア活動
vi....l volunteering

170 駅でチラシを配る
pass out fl..rs at the station

award
bulletin
celebrity
chief
coverage
dominated
editor
electronic
eminent
flyers
interrupt
journalism
person
publicity
virtual

一回で満点を取るより，何回もやってようやく満点を取る人の方が最後は勝つんだよ。
その方が頭の中の memory mechanism（記憶装置）にしっかり残るからだ。

Unit 4-2

フレーズ 161 個目から 170 個目までの答えをチェックしよう！　CD21

161 **editor-in-chief**
[édətər]

162 **meet a celebrity in person**
[səlébrəti]

163 **Royal wedding news dominated the headlines.**
[dámənèitid]

164 **an eminent, award*-winning writer**
[émənənt]　　[əwɔ́:rd] *発音注意。「アワード」ではなく「アウオード」。日本の報道機関などでは「アワード」と言っているところが多いが、これはとてもおかしい。

165 **put up publicity posters**
[pʌblísəti]

166 **electronic journalism**
[ilektránik]　[dʒə́:rnəlìzm]

167 **We interrupt this program for a special bulletin.**
[ìntərʌ́pt]　　　　　　　　　　　　　　[búlitən]

168 **wide coverage of the news**
[kʌ́vəridʒ]

169 **virtual volunteering**
[və́:rtʃuəl]　[vàləntíəriŋ]

170 **pass out flyers at the station**
[fláiərz]

点数チェック

/10　/10　/10　/10　/10　/10　/10　/10　/10　/10

Unit 4-3

道具・機器

左の欄から言葉を選んで……を完成しよう！

171 コンセントにトースターをつなぐ
p..g the toaster into the ou...t

172 基礎体温計（BBT）
ba..l body th........r (BBT)

173 家庭用電化器具
ho......d ap......es

174 冷凍庫の貯蔵能力
the storage ca.....y of a freezer

175 クリスマスツリーを飾るのに脚立(きゃたつ)を使う
use a st......er to decorate a Christmas tree

176 この複写機は1分間に100頁コピーする。
The ph.......er s..ts out 100 copies per minuite.

177 直線を描くには定規を使う
use a ru..r to draw a st.....t line

178 発光ダイオード（LED）
light em.....g diode (LED)

179 配管工事をする
install pl.....g

180 炊飯器にはタイマー予約機能がある。
The rice cooker has a de....d-start fu.....n.

appliances
basal
capacity
delayed
emitting
function
household
outlet
photocopier
plug
plumbing
ruler
spits
stepladder
straight
thermometer

一回で満点を取るより, 何回もやってようやく満点を取る人の方が最後は勝つんだよ。その方が頭の中の memory mechanism（記憶装置）にしっかり残るからだ。

Unit 4-3

フレーズ 171 個目から 180 個目までの答えをチェックしよう！ CD22

171 **plug the toaster into the outlet***
*コンセントは和製英語。[áutlet]

172 **basal body thermometer (BBT)**
[béisəl]　　　　　　[θərmámətər]

173 **household appliances**
[háushòuld]　　[əpláiənsiz]

174 **the storage capacity of a freezer**
[stɔ́:ridʒ]

175 **use a stepladder to decorate a Christmas tree**
[stéplæ̀dər]

176 **The photocopier spits out 100 copies per minute.**
[foutou-kápiər]

177 **use a ruler to draw a straight line**
[rú:lər]

178 **light emitting diode (LED)**
[imítiŋ]　　　[dáioud]

179 **install plumbing**
[plʌ́miŋ]

180 **The rice cooker has a delayed-start function.**
[fʌ́ŋkʃən]

点数チェック

Unit 4-4
健康と病気(2)

左の欄から言葉を選んで……を完成しよう！

181 喉(のど)が痛い
have a s..e throat

182 市販の風邪薬
over-the-c.....r cold me.....e

183 救急隊員
am......e c..w

184 意識を失う
lose co..........s

185 献血する
do...e blood

186 熱中症になる
suffer from he.......e

187 インフルエンザの流行
a flu ep.....c

188 歯を健康な状態に保つ
ma.....n good de...l health

189 転んで足首をねんざした
fell and sp.....d an an..e

190 気持ちが落ち込む
get de......d

ambulance
ankle
consciousness
counter
crew
dental
depressed
donate
epidemic
heatstroke
maintain
medicine
sore
sprained

一回で満点を取るより、何回もやってようやく満点を取る人の方が最後は勝つんだよ。その方が頭の中の memory mechanism（記憶装置）にしっかり残るからだ。

Unit 4-4

フレーズ 181 個目から 190 個目までの答えをチェックしよう！ CD23

181 **have a sore throat**
[sɔ́ːr] [θróut]

182 **over-the-counter* cold medicine**
*over-the-counter「薬局で処方箋なしで買える」という意味。[médəsin]

183 **ambulance crew**
[ǽmbjuləns]

184 **lose consciousness**
[kánʃəsnis] *同意語に faint, pass out もある。

185 **donate blood**
[dóuneit] [blʌ́d]

186 **suffer from heatstroke**
[híːtstrouk]

187 **a flu epidemic**
[èpədémik]

188 **maintain good dental health**
[meintéin]

189 **fell and sprained an ankle**
[spréind] [ǽŋkl]

190 **get depressed**
[diprést]

点数チェック

/10 /10 /10 /10 /10 /10 /10 /10 /10 /10

Unit 4-5

ビジネス・基礎編(3)

左の欄から言葉を選んで……を完成しよう!

191 営業時間は9時から5時です。
Bu.....s hours are 9 to 5.

192 草案を作る
draw up a dr..t plan

193 問い合わせには迅速に応える
quickly re....d to an in....y

194 新プロジェクトを認可する
au......e the new project

195 長い目で見れば費用効率がよい
cost-ef......e in the long r.n

196 任務を受けるよう説得する
pe.....e someone to take the assignment

197 士気(やる気)を保つ
keep the mo...e high

198 新入社員を仕事に慣れさせる
br..k in the new re.....s

199 指示に従う
fo...w the di......ns

200 提携会社
an af......e co........n

affiliate
authorize
break
business
corporation
directions
draft
effective
follow
inquiry
morale
persuade
recruits
respond
run

一回で満点を取るより, 何回もやってようやく満点を取る人の方が最後は勝つんだよ。その方が頭の中の memory mechanism (記憶装置) にしっかり残るからだ。

Unit 4-5

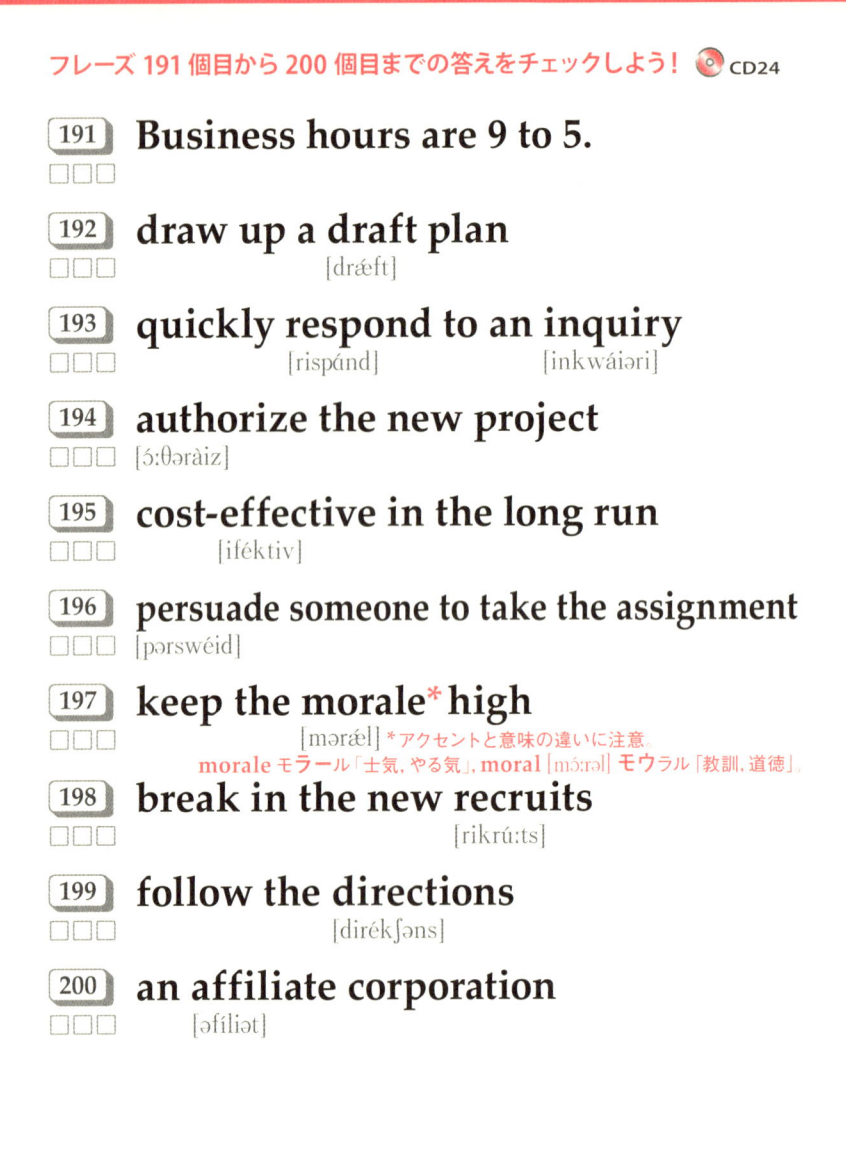

フレーズ 191 個目から 200 個目までの答えをチェックしよう！ CD24

191 Business hours are 9 to 5.

192 draw up a draft plan
[dræft]

193 quickly respond to an inquiry
[rispánd]   [inkwáiəri]

194 authorize the new project
[ɔ́:θəràiz]

195 cost-effective in the long run
[iféktiv]

196 persuade someone to take the assignment
[pərswéid]

197 keep the morale*high
[mərǽl] *アクセントと意味の違いに注意.
morale モラール「士気, やる気」, moral [mɔ́:rəl] モウラル「教訓, 道徳」.

198 break in the new recruits
[rikrú:ts]

199 follow the directions
[dirékʃəns]

200 an affiliate corporation
[əfíliət]

点数チェック

/10 /10 /10 /10 /10 /10 /10 /10 /10

Review Quiz for Unit 4 ▌75

ではここまで演習してきたら，君の記憶はかんぺきなはず。そこで Unit のおさらいをしよう。テキストを見ずに文の .... を埋められるかな？何度でも復習できるように，書き込みはせずにやってみよう。

ここにある文は，実際の「TOIEC Part 5 短文穴埋め問題」のものとほぼ同じ長さになっている。だからこの REVIEW QUIZ も TOEIC と同じペースで，1 問を 15 秒以内で答えるようにしよう。

1 回目は絶対に辞書を使わないこと！キーワードを拾って記憶で勝負！

必要に応じて，語形を変えることを忘れないように。
タイマーを 5 分に設定して，READY SET GO！   🔵 CD25

1. You shouldn't be .... the company's restructuring. I'm sure your job will be safe because it's one of the most important positions.

2. Sam looks as if he has a hangover. He must have .... too much drinking at the company party last night.

3. Tod took his assistant out for lunch to show her that he .... for losing his temper the other day.

4. On behalf of the entire company, we would like to apologize for making such ....

5. I can't believe I saw Lady Gigi! I've never seen .... before. Wow, was she gorgeous!

6. .... for our new washing detergent, Shine will be seen nationwide starting next week.

7. Quick, turn on the TV! There should be .... on Hurricane Paul.

8. .... makes it possible to help others without leaving your home or office.

9. Be sure to .... securely when you are using the vacuum cleaner.

10. These new energy-saving refrigerators are the best-sellers among our ....

11. The contractor is going to .... in our new house today. After that, we can start taking hot showers.

12. All rice cookers nowadays have .... So, when you come home in the evening, nice, hot, fluffy rice is waiting for you.

13. The receptionist can't answer the phones today. He has a bad .... and can't talk. Can someone take his place?

14. A: You'd better do something about that cold.
    B: Oh, it's not so bad. I'll just pick up some .... medicine at the drugstore.

15. Make sure you wear a hat and drink lots of water. You don't want to ....

16. I am so sorry about the delays. We are understaffed today as three out of five tellers are out today because of ....

17. Remember that it is most essential that you .... complaints from our customers as soon as possible.

18. Millie is a great salesperson! She can .... to buy these expensive Bucci bags.

19. A generous Christmas bonus will surely help to .... in the office.

Review Quiz for Unit 4   77

20. **Though our company wasn't involved in the tax evasion scandal caused by one of our .... , we were still embarrassed by it.**

    1. **Answer** concerned about
       会社のリストラについて君は心配要らないと思うよ。君の仕事は最重要な部署の一つだから安全だと思う。

    2. **Answer** indulged in
       サムは二日酔いみたいだ。きっと昨夜社のパーティでビールやらワインを飲み過ぎたんだね。

    3. **Answer** feels regretful
       トッドはこの間秘書を怒鳴ったことのお詫びのしるしに，彼女をランチに連れて行った。

    4. **Answer** a regrettable mistake
       このような残念な間違いを致しましたことを,全社を代表してお詫び申し上げます。

    5. **Answer** a celebrity in person
       信じられない！ レディー・ジジを見たよ。有名人を実際に見たのはこれが初めてだよ。彼女すごく素敵だった！

    6. **Answer** Publicity posters
       我が社の新洗剤,シャインの宣伝ポスターが来週から全国的に見られることになる。

    7. **Answer** a special bulletin
       急いでテレビをつけてごらん。ハリケーン・ポールに関するニュース速報をやっている。

    8. **Answer** Virtual volunteering
       ネットワーク上でするボランティアの仕事は，家やオフィスにいながら人助けが出来る。

    9. **Answer** plug it into the outlet
       掃除機を使うときは，コードをしっかり電源に差し込んで下さい。

    10. **Answer** household appliances
        この省エネタイプの新型冷蔵庫は,現在私どもでベストセラーの家電商品です。

11. **Answer** install the plumbing
    工務店が今日家の配管工事をする。その後，熱いシャワーが浴びられるようになるよ。

12. **Answer** a delayed-start function
    最近の炊飯器には全てタイマー予約が付いている。だから，夜帰宅すると，ほかほかご飯が待っているんだ。

13. **Answer** sore throat
    本日受付係は電話の応対が出来ません。彼は喉を痛めていて，声が出ないので。誰か代わってやってくれませんか。

14. **Answer** over-the-counter
    A: その風邪なんとか手当てしなよ。
    B: それほど酷くないんだ。薬屋で，売薬を買うことにするよ。

15. **Answer** suffer from heatstroke
    必ず帽子をかぶって水をたくさん飲もう。熱中症にかからないようにね。

16. **Answer** the flu epidemic
    お待たせして申し訳ありません。インフルエンザの流行で，５人の窓口係のうち３人が休みなので手が足りないのです。

17. **Answer** respond to
    出来る限り迅速に顧客の苦情に対応することが，最重要だと言うことを忘れないように。

18. **Answer** persuade anyone
    ミリーは素晴らしい販売員だ！ 彼女はどんな人でもこの高価なブッチのバッグを買う気にさせる。

19. **Answer** keep the morale high
    高額のクリスマスボーナスは，おおいにオフィスの士気を高めるのに役立つよ。

20. **Answer** affiliate corporations
    我が社は関連会社が起こした脱税スキャンダルに関わっていなかったが，やはり恥ずかしく思った。

Power Builder Chart

| /20 | /20 | /20 | /20 | /20 | /20 | /20 | /20 | /20 | /20 |

黒猫トントンのちょっとブレイク 4

**Emotions and Feelings
有頂天からまっさかさま!**

きのう, 黒猫トントンは珍しくきちんと **completed his assignment** 宿題をやってきて, それがまた **got 100 % correct** 全部正解だったので, **He got a slap on the back** オーガにほめられた。それで **Ton Ton was feeling on top of the world** 彼は有頂天だったんだ。

でも, 当然トントンのような **moody and impulsive cat** とうとつで気まぐれ猫は **can't keep up one's high spirits** やる気がつづくはずもなく, 今日はトントン **did a disappearing act** 雲を霞とどこかへ行ってしまい, **played hooky from Ooga's class.** オーガのクラスをさぼったんだ。

人間は知らないけど, 猫には **millions of complex feelings** 数えきれないほどの複雑な感情があるのよね。そして, 人間だって猫ほど複雑じゃないけど **some emotions and feelings** いくつかの感情があるのさ。

人も状況によって, 色々な感情を持つよね。その人の性格がどうであろうと, 状況に対する感情にはかなりの共通点がある。いくつかのケースでの **emotional expressions** 感情の表現を読んでみよう。

感情の表現：emotional expressions

Case 1

明日は就職試験だ	Jim feels anxious and can't fall asleep. 心配で眠れない。
就職試験の直前	Jim is nervous and has stage fright. 心配であがっている。
面接官たちの前で	Jim tries to stay calm and behave rationally. 平静さを保ち理性的に行動するよう努める。
面接の後で	Jim feels so relieved but he's also exhausted. どっと安心して疲れる。
翌日採用の電話をもらう	Jim feels exalted and shouts with glee. 大喜びで叫び出す。

Case 2

プロジェクト案が却下された	Helen feels disappointed and discouraged. 失望してがっかり。
もう一度やり直そう	Helen looks it over cautiously and meticulously. プランをもう一度注意深く，細かく見直す。
チームで検討する	Helen appreciates her supportive teammates. 支えてくれて協力的なチームメイトに感謝。
第2案は満場一致で採用	Helen feels satisfied and rewarded. とても満足で報われた感じ。

Case 3

兄が戦死したという突然の悲報	**Lynn was devastated.** リンはショックを受け，打ちのめされた。
葬儀の準備をする	**Lynn reluctantly but dutifully followed the procedure.** 仕方なく義務的に決められた式次第に従った。
棺は埋葬された	**Lynn's grief was so fierce that she went into a frenzy of rage against the country that killed her brother.** あまりの激しい悲しみに，リンは兄を殺した国に対して激しく怒る。
1年後	**Lynn feels calmer but still deeply sad when she visits her brother's grave.** リンは少し落ち着いたものの，未だ深い悲しみを持って兄の墓に参る。

Don't be emotional!

Touchy Points

ある国際会議場でスピーチをした外交官のお話。

あまり得意でない英語で、訳の分からんことを言ったので、出席者からの失笑を買った。彼、頭に来て、*"Don't Laugh! Shut up."* と怒鳴ってしまったの。これは、すっごく失礼なことで、こういう国際会議場で、命令形で怒鳴るなどというのはもってのほか。くだらないことを言えば失笑をかうのは当たり前。それでもどうしても、逆切れして注意したいのなら *"Would you mind not laughing at me? You are making me very nervous."* 「笑わないでいただけませんか。とてもあがってしまうのです。」とでも言うべきだったかも。

とにかく、この人物の外交官としてのキャリアがこのとき終わったのはほぼ確実なことね。

Unit 5-1

日常生活

左の欄から言葉を選んで……を完成しよう！

201 朝の日課をすませる
go through a morning ro....e

202 口をゆすいで，うがいをする
ri..e your mouth and ga...e

203 いらつく通勤電車
an ag........g co.....r train

204 書店でぶらぶら時間をつぶす
k..l time by br.....g in a bookstore

205 粗大ゴミを捨てる
throw out the ru....h

206 コインランドリーで洗濯する
do the la....y at a Laundromat

207 芝刈り機で草を刈る
cut the grass with a lawn m...r

208 料理持ち寄りでパーティをする
have a po....k party

209 床に掃除機をかける
va...m the floor

210 ひどい馬鹿騒ぎをする
ra..e a terrible ra...t

aggravating
browsing
commuter
gargle
kill
laundry
mower
potluck
racket
raise
rinse
routine
rubbish
vacuum

一回で満点を取るより，何回もやってようやく満点を取る人の方が最後は勝つんだよ。
その方が頭の中の memory mechanism（記憶装置）にしっかり残るからだ。

Unit 5-1

フレーズ 201 個目から 210 個目までの答えをチェックしよう！ CD26

201 go through a morning routine
[ruːtíːn]

202 rinse your mouth and gargle
[gáːrgl]

203 an aggravating commuter train
[ǽgrəvèitiŋ] [kəmjúːtər]

204 kill time by browsing in a bookstore
[bráuziŋ]

205 throw out the rubbish
[rʌ́biʃ]

206 do the laundry at a Laundromat*
[lɔ́ːndri]
*Laundromat（コインランドリー）は商標だが、今は普通名詞としても使われている。
欧米の高層住宅では各戸に洗濯機を置けないところが多いので Laundromat で洗濯する。

207 cut the grass with a lawn mower
[móuər]

208 have a potluck party
[pátlʌk]

209 vacuum the floor
[vǽkjuəm]

210 raise a terrible racket
[térəbl] [rǽkit]

点数チェック

/10 /10 /10 /10 /10 /10 /10 /10 /10 /10

Unit 5-2

エネルギー・発電

左の欄から言葉を選んで……を完成しよう！

211 エネルギーを節約する方法を学ぶ
learn to co.....e energy

212 高圧電線に注意！
Watch out for high vo....e power lines!

213 水は悪影響ゼロのエネルギー源。
Water is a zero-im...t energy so...e.

214 自給自足のソーラーハウス
self-su.......g solar homes

215 大停電
a ma....e bl.....t

blackout
conserve
fossil
fuel
hydraulic
hydrogen
impact
massive
potential
source
static
sustaining
unlimited
voltage

216 水素エネルギーの自動車
hy.....n-powered automobiles

217 化石燃料から出る廃棄物
fo...l f..l waste

218 水力発電所
a hy......c power plant

219 静電気防止スプレー
st...c-free spray

220 風力発電の限りない可能性
wind power's unli....d po......l

一回で満点を取るより，何回もやってようやく満点を取る人の方が最後は勝つんだよ。その方が頭の中の memory mechanism（記憶装置）にしっかり残るからだ。

Unit 5-2

フレーズ 211 個目から 220 個目までの答えをチェックしよう！　CD27

211 **learn to conserve energy***
[kənsə́ːrv] [énərdʒi]
*energyは発音とアクセント両方ができないと通じない。しっかりshadowing練習すること。

212 **Watch out for high voltage power lines!**
[vóultidʒ]

213 **Water is a zero-impact energy source.**
[ímpækt]

214 **self-sustaining solar homes**
[səstéiniŋ]

215 **a massive blackout**
[mǽsiv]

216 **hydrogen-powered automobiles**
[háidrədʒən]

217 **fossil fuel* waste**
[fásəl] *fossil fuel … 石油,石炭,天然ガスなど化石燃料

218 **a hydraulic power plant**
[haidrɔ́ːlik]

219 **static-free spray**
[stǽtik]

220 **wind power's unlimited potential**
[pəténʃəl]

点数チェック

/10　/10　/10　/10　/10　/10　/10　/10　/10　/10

Unit 5-3

公共交通

左の欄から言葉を選んで……を完成しよう！

221 病院区域につきクラクション禁止
No Ho....g! Hospital Zone

222 通行止め
a tr....c ban

223 老人・障害者のための優先席
pr.....y seats for the elderly and di.....d

224 歩行者天国
a ve....e-free promenade

225 豪華な大陸横断列車で旅する
travel by lu......s trans-co........l train

226 ニューヨーク–ボストン間の短距離便
a sh....e f....t from New York to Boston

227 交通費を支給する
provide a tr..........n al......e

228 渋滞を緩和する
ease the co.......n

229 タクシーを呼び止める
h..l a cab

230 電車内の緊急警報装置
the train's em......y al..m system

alarm
allowance
congestion
continental
disabled
emergency
flight
hail
honking
luxurious
priority
shuttle
traffic
transportation
vehicle

一回で満点を取るより, 何回もやってようやく満点を取る人の方が最後は勝つんだよ。その方が頭の中の memory mechanism (記憶装置) にしっかり残るからだ。

Unit 5-3

フレーズ 221 個目から 230 個目までの答えをチェックしよう！ CD28

221 No Honking! Hospital Zone
[háŋkiŋ]

222 a traffic ban
[trǽfik]

223 priority seats for the elderly and disabled
[praió:rəti]　　　　　　　　　　　　　[diséibld]

224 a vehicle-free promenade
[víːikl]　　　　　[pràmənéid]

225 travel by luxurious trans-continental train
[lʌgʒúəriəs]

226 a shuttle flight from New York to Boston
[ʃʌ́tl]

227 provide a transportation allowance
[trænspərtéiʃən]　　　　[əláuəns]

228 ease the congestion
[kəndʒéstʃən]

229 hail a cab
[héil]

230 the train's emergency alarm system
[imə́ːrdʒənsi]　　[əláːrm]

点数チェック

Unit 5-4

健康と栄養

左の欄から言葉を選んで……を完成しよう！

231 長寿食療法に従う
follow a ma........c diet

232 肥満度指数を低く保とう。
Keep your body-m..s in..x low.

233 不規則な食習慣
er....c eating habits

234 ダイエットにやさしいソース類
diet-fr.....y sauces

235 体重減量プログラム
a weight-re......n program

236 タンパク質の多い食物をとる
eat high-pr....n foods

237 一日のカロリー摂取量（せっしゅりょう）を計算する
c...t your daily calorie in...e

238 良い食事をして体型を維持する
eat well and keep in sh..e

239 摂食障害（せっしょくしょうがい）がある
have an ea...g di.....r

240 栄養的要素を考慮する
take nu.......al fa...rs into account

count
disorder
eating
erratic
factors
friendly
index
intake
macrobiotic
mass
nutritional
protein
reduction
shape

一回で満点を取るより、何回もやってようやく満点を取る人の方が最後は勝つんだよ。
その方が頭の中の memory mechanism（記憶装置）にしっかり残るからだ。

Unit 5-4

フレーズ 231 個目から 240 個目までの答えをチェックしよう！ CD29

231 follow a macrobiotic diet
[mæ̀kroubaiɑ́tik]

232 Keep your body-mass index low.
[índeks]

233 erratic eating habits
[irǽtik]

234 diet-friendly sauces
[sɔ́ːsz]

235 a weight-reduction program
[ridʌ́kʃən]

236 eat high-protein foods
[próutiːn]

237 count your daily calorie intake
[kǽləri]

238 eat well and keep in shape*
*同義語 … stay (keep) in shape 反対語 … get (be) out of shape 体型が崩れる

239 have an eating disorder
[disɔ́ːrdər]

240 take nutritional factors into account
[njuːtríʃənl]

点数チェック

/10 /10 /10 /10 /10 /10 /10 /10 /10 /10

Unit 5-5

ビジネス・基礎編(4)

左の欄から言葉を選んで……を完成しよう！

241 あまり良くない勤務評価
a me.....e performance record

242 消費者意見アンケートに記入する
fill out a consumer fe.....k qu..........e

243 旅費を負担する
cover travel ex........es

244 誠実な顧客に報いるための特別提供品
a special offer to re...d lo..l clients

additional
close
deal
development
distinguished
expenditures
feedback
handling
infrastructure
loyal
mediocre
questionnaire
reward
safety
tactics

245 キャリア開発セミナー
career-de........t seminar

246 傑出した実業家
a di..........d businessperson

247 売り込み戦略を練る
work on sales ta...cs

248 商談を成立させる
cl..e a business d..l

249 安全のための基幹施設を構築する
establish a sa...y in..........e

250 送料と手数料は別途
ad.......l shipping and ha.....g charges

一回で満点を取るより，何回もやってようやく満点を取る人の方が最後は勝つんだよ。その方が頭の中の memory mechanism（記憶装置）にしっかり残るからだ。

Unit 5-5

フレーズ 241 個目から 250 個目までの答えをチェックしよう！　CD30

241 a mediocre performance record
[mìːdióukər]　[pərfɔ́ːrməns]

242 fill out a consumer feedback questionnaire
[kənsúːmər]　[kwèstʃənéər]

243 cover travel expenditures
[ikspénditʃərs]

244 a special offer to reward loyal clients
[riwɔ́ːrd]

245 career*-development seminar
[kəríər]　[divéləpmənt]
*アクセント注意。「キャリア」ではなく、「クリーア」

246 a distinguished businessperson
[distíŋgwiʃt]

247 work on sales tactics
[tǽktiks]

248 close* a business deal
[klóuz] *発音注意。動詞は「クローズ」、形容詞「近い」は「クロース」。

249 establish a safety infrastructure
[ínfrəstrʌ́ktʃər]

250 additional shipping and handling charges
[ədíʃənl]

点数チェック

| /10 | /10 | /10 | /10 | /10 | /10 | /10 | /10 | /10 | /10 |

Review Quiz for Unit 5　93

ではここまで演習してきたら，君の記憶はかんぺきなはず。そこでUnitのおさらいをしよう。テキストを見ずに文の............を埋められるかな？何度でも復習できるように，書き込みはせずにやってみよう。

ここにある文は，実際の「TOIEC Part 5 短文穴埋め問題」のものとほぼ同じ長さになっている。だからこのREVIEW QUIZもTOEICと同じペースで，1問を15秒以内で答えるようにしよう。

1回目は絶対に辞書を使わないこと！ キーワードを拾って記憶で勝負！

必要に応じて，語形を変えることを忘れないように。
タイマーを5分に設定して，READY SET GO！　　CD31

1. Making coffee and checking his email are part of Allan's .... at the office.

2. I'll miss my coworkers after I retire next month, but I won't miss riding that .... every morning.

3. After the spring cleaning, we ended up with lots of old shoes and clothes we don't use anymore. What day do we .... ?

4. Jim is going to bake a pineapple upside-down cake to take to the .... at church next Sunday.

5. We can .... if we replace all the automatic doors in this building with regular manual doors.

6. And the best part about this new vegetable-growing process is that it will have .... on the environment.

7. This .... keeps me from getting an electric shock every time I touch the doorknob.

8. The cellphone market in this country has .... for expansion.

9. It's a lot quieter around here on Sundays ever since they started ....

10. The young man kept on sitting in .... even though an elderly woman with a cane came on board.

11. There's .... leaving for Seattle from San Jose every hour on the hour.

12. Don't forget to hand in the request form or you won't get your .... for your commute.

13. .... diet was developed in Japan based on traditional vegetarian cooking.

14. The doctor told Charlene that she has to change her .... and eat more regular meals.

15. Try EZ LOSE products for low-calorie .... snacks.

16. Have you noticed how thin Yumiko has gotten? I wonder if she has ....

17. Dale's .... is what's keeping him from being promoted.

18. .... indicates that our target age group has responded negatively to our new TV commercial.

19. Donald would be more successful with potential customers if his .... weren't so aggressive.

20. The most urgent task for the city is to build an effective system of .... to prepare for the expected big earthquake.

Review Quiz for Unit 5

1. **Answer** morning routine
   コーヒーを入れてメールをチェックするのがオフィスでのアランの朝の日課です。

2. **Answer** aggravating commuter train
   来月退職したら、同僚たちに会えないのはさびしいけど、毎朝の頭に来る電車通勤が無くなってほっとするよ。

3. **Answer** throw out the rubbish
   春の大掃除の後、もう要らない大量の古靴と衣類が出たんだ。次の廃品ゴミを捨てる日はいつ？

4. **Answer** potluck party
   ジムは教会の持ち寄りパーティに「逆さまパインケーキ」を焼いていくつもりだ。

5. **Answer** conserve energy
   このビル中の自動ドアをすべて手動式に代えれば、エネルギーを節約できるよ。

6. **Answer** zero impact
   この新野菜栽培法の最大の長所は、環境への悪影響が一切無いということです。

7. **Answer** static-free spray
   この静電気防止スプレーは、ドアを触るたびに襲う静電気ショックを防いでくれる。

8. **Answer** unlimited potential
   この国での携帯電話市場は発展の可能性が限りなくある。

9. **Answer** the traffic ban
   日曜の通行止めが始まって以来、ここら辺はずっと静かになった。

10. **Answer** the priority seat
    その若者は杖をついた年配の女性が乗車して来たにもかかわらず、優先席に座り続けた。

11. **Answer** a shuttle flight
    シアトルからサンホセへの往復便は毎時丁度に出発します。

12. **Answer** transportation allowance
    申請書を提出するのを忘れないで。でないと通勤手当をもらえないよ。

13. **Answer** The macrobiotic food
    長寿食は伝統的な菜食料理をもとにして，日本で発達した食事法です。

14. **Answer** erratic eating habits
    シャーリーンは不規則な食習慣を変えて規則的な食事をしなければ，体重を減らせないだろうと医者は言った。

15. **Answer** diet-friendly
    低カロリーで，ダイエットに優しい，イージー・ルーズのスナック製品をどうぞ。

16. **Answer** an eating disorder
    ユミコはすごくやせたと思わない？ 摂食障害になっているのじゃないかな。

17. **Answer** mediocre performance record
    デールの勤務評価はあまり良くなくて，昇進の邪魔になっている。

18. **Answer** The consumer feedback questionnaire
    消費者意見調査によると，わが社が目標としている年齢層は，新しいテレビコマーシャルについて否定的な反応を示した。

19. **Answer** sales tactics
    ドナルドは見込み客に対してあまり積極的すぎる売り込み戦術でないほうが，うまくいくと思う。

20. **Answer** safety infrastructure
    市の現在の最重要課題は，予期される大地震に備えて有効な安全のための基盤組織を構築することだ。

Power Builder Chart

| /20 | /20 | /20 | /20 | /20 | /20 | /20 | /20 | /20 | /20 |

黒猫トントンのちょっとブレイク 5

Suffixes "-holics," "-friendly," "-free"
おもしろい接尾語たち

オーガ： Hey, Ton Ton, what's the matter with you? Why are you waddling around どうしたの？ 何でそんなによたよたしてんだい？ おまけに drooling all over よだれ，たれまくってるじゃないか。まるで You look like our alcoholic grandpa アルコール依存症の爺さんみたいだよ。

トントン： ウ〜イ，I found some nice-smelling leaves this morning. 今朝，匂いのいい木の葉っぱをみつけたの。食べたら can't stop drooling よだれが出てとまらなくなったっス。ウ〜イ, slovering, slovering シャバシャバッ！

オーガ： そうか，分かった。トントン，お前きっと silver vine 「またたび」を食べたんだ。cat's favorite vine plant 猫が大好きなつる科の植物で，食べると cats become drunk 酔っぱらっちゃうんだ。

トントン： Don't know why but I feel so Gooood. ZZZ... なんだかしらないけど，良い気持ちダーイ。オーガシェンシェイ，オヤスミー。**グー**……

で，今回は **"-holic," "-free," "-friendly"** など接尾語のつく言葉について一席。

1. -holic のつく言葉

もともと **"Alcoholic"** という言葉は **"alcohol"** に形容を表す **"-ic"** がついたもので，**alcoholic beverage**「アルコールの飲料」という意味で使われていた。それが，150年ほど前から，**a person who is addicted to drinking alcoholic beverages,** すなわちアルコール中毒者を表す意味に使われるようになった。

他にも **holic** のつく言葉がここから発生した。

coffeeholic	コーヒー中毒
chocoholic	チョコレート中毒
sugarholic	甘いもの中毒
workaholic	働き中毒
shopaholic	買い物中毒
danceaholic	ダンス中毒
sexaholic	セックス中毒

最後の **sexaholic** は耳なれない言葉かもしれないが，じっさいにかなり **serious symptoms** 深刻な症状を持つ人たちがあり，**Alcoholics Anonymous**「アルコール中毒者更正会」のように **Sexaholics Anonymous**「セックス中毒者匿名会」という会がある。

2. friendly は形容詞です

最近多く新聞，雑誌記事で見る言葉に，**friendly** があるよね。これはとても **tricky** な言葉だから，気を付けよう。

FRIENDLY に関する三つのワナ 😎

ワナ 1.
-ly がついても **friendly** は普通は副詞ではなく形容詞。おまけに，比較級，最上級が **friendlier, friendliest** などと変化するというクセモノだ。だから，**TOEIC** や他の英語能力試験の出題者にとっては嬉しくてたまらん言葉なの。

ワナ 2.
この **friendly** にぴったりあった日本語訳は難しい。**situation** 状況によって「**gentle, warm, easy-going, kind, easy-to-use, protective** 優しい，暖かい，気さくな，親切な，使いやすい，保護する」などといろいろな意味を持つ。次にくる名詞で訳も考えよう。

ワナ 3.
最大に気を付けるべきことは，**friendly** が名詞の前に来たときと，後に来たときには全く意味が違うということ。

friendly dog ...　　　　　人なつこい犬
dog-friendly park ...　　　犬も入れる公園

ここでは，**mass media** や **TOEIC** によくでる **friendly** が後につく言葉を覚えよう。

age-friendly city　　　　　　高齢者に優しい都市
access-friendly software　　使い易いソフト
battery-friendly flashlight　消費電力が少ない懐中電灯
child-friendly community　　子供に優しい地域社会
diet-friendly sauce　　　　　ダイエットに良いソース
customer-friendly price　　　客が買いやすい値段
eco-friendly farming　　　　環境を保護する農業
user-friendly appliance　　　使い易い器具

3. free drinks, smoke-free の落とし穴!

最後に free という言葉について。これも，またまた，前につくか後ろにつくかでまったく意味が違ってくるのよね。free が始めに来ると，「無料の，自由な」という意味になり，後に来ると，「禁止の，〜の無い」という意味になるので注意。

free food and drinks provided	無料の食べ物とドリンク
free brochures	無料のパンフレット
vehicle-free promenade	歩行者天国
smoke-free area	喫煙禁止区域
contamination-free area	非汚染地域

Touchy Points

オーガの友人で heavily addicted smoker ヘビースモーカーの男性が，ニューヨークに出張したときの話。フライト中の10数時間も含めて全て "No Smoking" sign 禁煙サインばかりで，彼，もう，ものすごい欲求不満になっちまった！ でも，Kennedy Airport を出たとたん，急にニコニコ，He quickly took out a cigarette and was about to light it さっとタバコをとりだし，その速いこと速いこと，あわや火を付けようとしたとき，airport security guard jumped on him 空港警備のおいちゃんがとんできて，止められてしまった。Outraged, pointing at the sign, he yelled, "Smoke-Free Area." 彼，憤懣(ふんまん)やるかたなく，そこで一発，サインを指さして，「"タバコを自由に吸える所"と書いてあるやんけー。」と怒鳴ったんだけどねー。

Unit 6-1

家族・人生

左の欄から言葉を選んで……を完成しよう！

- anniversary
- birth
- birthrate
- certificate
- chip
- companion
- declining
- descendant
- downs
- expectant
- hand
- license
- marriage
- resemblance
- shower

251 市役所で出生証明書をとる
get a bi..h ce……e at City Hall

252 結婚するには結婚許可証が必要
need a ma…..e li….e to get married

253 家族（伴侶）としての動物と暮らす
live with a co……n animal

254 妊娠中の女性
an ex……t mother

255 皆で出し合って出産祝いをする
c..p in on a baby sh…r

256 姉からのお下がり
h..d-me-do..s from my elder sister

257 ワン家の子孫
a de……t of the Wong family

258 金婚式を祝う
celebrate a golden wedding an……ry

259 低下しつつある出生率
a de…..g bi……e

260 家族として似ている点がある
carry a family re……e

一回で満点を取るより, 何回もやってようやく満点を取る人の方が最後は勝つんだよ。その方が頭の中の memory mechanism（記憶装置）にしっかり残るからだ。

Unit 6-1

フレーズ 251 個目から 260 個目までの答えをチェックしよう！ CD32

251 get a birth certificate at City Hall
[sərtífikət]

252 need a marriage license to get married
[mǽridʒ] *p113 〜エッセイ参照

253 live with a companion animal
[kəmpǽnjən]

254 an expectant mother
[ikspéktənt]

255 chip in on a baby shower
[tʃíp]

256 hand-me-downs from my elder sister
[éldər]

257 a descendant of the Wong family
[diséndənt]

258 celebrate a golden wedding anniversary
[séləbrèit]

259 a declining birthrate
[dikláiniŋ]

260 carry a family resemblance
[rizémbləns]

点数チェック
/10 /10 /10 /10 /10 /10 /10 /10 /10 /10

Unit 6-2

美術・芸術

左の欄から言葉を選んで……を完成しよう！

261 さわって体験できる博物館
a ha..s-on museum

262 セザンヌ展への招待状
an invitation to the Cezanne ex....t

263 実物大の彫刻
a life-size sc......e

264 美術館の学芸員・館長
the cu....r of an art museum

265 聖書から啓示を受けた傑作
a ma........e in.....d by the Bible

266 公開予定の催（もよお）しの発表
an.........t of up.....g events

267 オペラの歴史的背景
the hi.......l ba.......d of the opera

268 石器時代の原始芸術
pr......e art of the Stone Age

269 考古学博物館
a museum of ar.......y

270 本物のゴヤの絵
an au......c painting by Goya

announcement
archeology
authentic
background
curator
exhibit
hands
historical
inspired
masterpiece
primitive
sculpture
upcoming

一回で満点を取るより，何回もやってようやく満点を取る人の方が最後は勝つんだよ。
その方が頭の中の memory mechanism（記憶装置）にしっかり残るからだ。

Unit 6-2

フレーズ 261 個目から 270 個目までの答えをチェックしよう！　CD33

261 a hands-on museum
[mju:zí:əm]

262 an invitation to the Cezanne exhibit
[igzíbit]

263 a life-size sculpture
[skʌ́lptʃər]

264 the curator of an art museum
[kjuəréitər]

265 a masterpiece inspired by the Bible
[mǽstərpi:s] [inspáiərd]

266 announcement of upcoming events
[ənáunsmənt]

267 the historical background of the opera
[histɔ́:rikəl]

268 primitive art of the Stone Age
[prímətiv]

269 the museum of archeology
[à:rkiálədʒi]

270 an authentic painting by Goya
[ɔ:θéntik]

点数チェック

Unit 6-3

外食・レストラン

左の欄から言葉を選んで……を完成しよう！

271 急いで食事をとる
grab a qu..k b..e

272 出張料理を手配する
make ca.....g ar........ts

273 きちんと説明のできるウエイター
a well-in.....d waitperson

274 残った料理のための犬用バッグ
a doggy bag for le.....rs

275 晩餐会のため正装する
dress fo....ly for a ba....t

appetizer
arrangements
banquet
bite
catering
favorite
formally
helping
informed
leftovers
mouthwatering
quick
review
sampler

276 気に入ったレストランをひいきにする
frequent a fa.....e restaurant

277 前菜盛り合わせを注文する
order an ap......r s.....r

278 食欲をそそるビュッフェランチ
a mo.........ng buffet lunch

279 おかわりをする
ask for a second he....g

280 レストラン評をチェックする
check the restaurant re...w

一回で満点を取るより，何回もやってようやく満点を取る人の方が最後は勝つんだよ。その方が頭の中の memory mechanism（記憶装置）にしっかり残るからだ。

Unit 6-3

フレーズ 271 個目から 280 個目までの答えをチェックしよう！ CD34

271 **grab a quick bite**
[græb] [báit]

272 **make catering arrangements**
[kéitəriŋ]

273 **a well-informed waitperson**
[infɔ́:rmd]

274 **a doggy bag* for leftovers**
[léftouvərz]
*必ずしも犬用でなくても、doggy bag という言い方をする。

275 **dress formally for a banquet**
[bǽŋkwit]

276 **frequent a favorite restaurant**
[frikwént] [féivərit]

277 **order an appetizer sampler**
[ǽpətàizər]

278 **a mouthwatering buffet lunch**
[máuθwɔ̀:təríŋ] [bəféi] *アクセント注意。「バッ**フェ**」

279 **ask for a second helping***
*レストランでの食事や招待されたときのおかわり。second serving ともいう。

280 **check the restaurant review**
[rivjú:]

点数チェック

Unit 6-4
政治・選挙

左の欄から言葉を選んで......を完成しよう！

281 選挙対策本部
ca.....n he........rs

282 革新派のリーダー
a pr........e leader

283 投票の結果
ou....e of the ba...t

284 政府の報道官
a sp.........n for the government

285 助成金を申請する
apply for a su...y

286 総理大臣として指名をとる
win the no.......n for prime minister

287 内閣支持率
ca....t ap.....l rating

288 世論動向調査
a tr..d-tracking p..l

289 収賄を否定する
d..y accepting br....y

290 厳しい危機に対処する
c..e with a tough cr...s

approval
ballot
bribery
cabinet
campaign
cope
crisis
deny
headquarters
nomination
outcome
poll
progressive
spokesperson
subsidy
trend

一回で満点を取るより，何回もやってようやく満点を取る人の方が最後は勝つんだよ。その方が頭の中の memory mechanism（記憶装置）にしっかり残るからだ。

Unit 6-4

フレーズ 281 個目から 290 個目までの答えをチェックしよう！ CD35

281 **campaign headquarters***
[hédkwɔːrtərz] *headquaters「本部・本店」は普通複数扱い。

282 **a progressive leader**
[prəgrésiv]

283 **outcome of the ballot**
[bǽlət]

284 **a spokesperson for the government**
[spóukspəːrsn]

285 **apply for a subsidy**
[sʌ́bsədi]

286 **win the nomination for prime minister**
[nàmənéiʃən]

287 **cabinet approval rating**
[əprúːvəl]

288 **a trend-tracking poll**
[póul]

289 **deny accepting* bribery**
[dinái]　　　　　[bráibəri] *deny + ~ing の形を取る

290 **cope with a tough crisis**
[kráisis]

点数チェック
/10　/10　/10　/10　/10　/10　/10　/10　/10

Unit 6-5

ビジネス・基礎編(5)

左の欄から言葉を選んで……を完成しよう！

291 良い評判を得る
earn a good re.......n

292 貿易摩擦を解決する努力をする
try to re....e the trade co.....t

293 技術提携の契約をする
sign a te......l af........n agreement

294 通達事項を掲示板に貼りだす
post a no...e on the bu.....n board

295 衰退期をうまく乗り切る
succeed in ov.......g the sl..p

296 添付書類をごらん下さい。
See the attached do.....t.

297 広報部
pu...c re......s department

298 運送業者
a fo.......g agent

299 30%の利幅を維持する
ma.....n a 30% profit m....n

300 新製品を売り出す
la...h a new product

affiliation
bulletin
conflict
document
forwarding
launch
maintain
margin
notice
overcoming
public
relations
reputation
resolve
slump
technical

一回で満点を取るより, 何回もやってようやく満点を取る人の方が最後は勝つんだよ。その方が頭の中の memory mechanism (記憶装置) にしっかり残るからだ。

Unit 6-5

フレーズ 291 個目から 300 個目までの答えをチェックしよう！ CD36

291 earn a good reputation
[rèpjutéiʃən]

292 try to resolve the trade conflict
[rizálv] [kánflikt]

293 sign a technical affiliation agreement
[téknikəl] [əfìliéiʃən]

294 post a notice on the bulletin board
[búlitn]

295 succeed in overcoming the slump
[səksí:d] [slʌ́mp]

296 See the attached document.
[ətǽtʃt]

297 public relations department
[riléiʃənz]

298 a forwarding* agent
[fɔ́:rwərdiŋ] *syn. forwarder

299 maintain a 30% profit margin
[meintéin]

300 launch a new product
[lɔ́:ntʃ]

点数チェック

Review Quiz for Unit 6

ではここまで演習してきたら，君の記憶はかんぺきなはず。そこでUnitのおさらいをしよう。テキストを見ずに文の............を埋められるかな？何度でも復習できるように，書き込みはせずにやってみよう。

ここにある文は，実際の「TOIEC Part 5 短文穴埋め問題」のものとほぼ同じ長さになっている。だからこのREVIEW QUIZ も TOEIC と同じペースで，1問を15秒以内で答えるようにしよう。

1回目は絶対に辞書を使わないこと！キーワードを拾って記憶で勝負！

必要に応じて，語形を変えることを忘れないように。
タイマーを5分に設定して，READY SET GO！

CD37

1. Tomorrow is going to be a busy day. After we get our .... at City Hall, we have an appointment with the wedding planner, and then I have a fitting for my wedding gown.

2. Marie is attending a special class for .... because she wants to give birth without using any drugs.

3. A: Is Tracey coming with us to the used-clothing boutique?
   B: No. She says she has two older sisters and is tired of wearing ....

4. It's easy to see that he's your brother since .... is so strong.

5. Let's take our kids to the new science museum. I'm sure they will really enjoy trying out all the .... exhibits.

6. One of the things that I really like about working in the mayor's office is that I get .... that come to town.

7. The inventor who spoke at our school last week said that he was .... reading about people like Thomas Edison and Alexander Graham Bell.

8. That picture was stored in the museum's basement for years until someone noticed that it was .... by Matisse.

9. If we go to Charlene's dance performance directly from work, do you think we'll have to .... on the way?

10. I used to .... neighborhood movie theater at least once a week before they tore it down.

11. Well, I'll certainly have to start my diet tomorrow after taking .... of everything at the office Christmas party.

12. Let's take our new clients to Kevin's Steak House. I heard that it received an excellent .... from a famous food critic.

13. .... is now clearly in favor of our candidate. So let's head for the campaign headquarters and get ready for the victory celebration.

14. If we .... from the city, we can convert the headquarters building to solar energy and cut our electricity bill by 30%.

15. My responsibility is to analyze various .... and based on what we find, determine what new products we should be developing.

16. Shunichi has only worked here for three months but he really .... the pressure of meeting clients well, doesn't he?

17. After working hard to improve the quality of our products, we have .... in the vitamin and supplement industry.

18. If the Engineering Department can .... a couple of minor software problems, our company will be the first to market a robot that can recognize faces.

19. We have 250 bags of rice to be delivered to our wholesaler by Monday. Make sure our .... picks them up for delivery today.

Review Quiz for Unit 6   113

20. A: Oooh, what's that lovely smell?
    B: Well, it's us. We just came back from a press release party held by a fragrance maker who is ....

1. **Answer** marriage license
   明日は忙しい日になるわ。市役所で結婚許可証をとってから、結婚プランナーと約束、それから私のドレスの仮縫いがあるから。

2. **Answer** expectant mothers
   マリーは、薬を使わず出産できるように、妊婦のための特別クラスに出る予定だ。

3. **Answer** hand-me-downs
   A: トレーシーは古着ブティックに一緒に来るの？
   B: いや、彼女は二人お姉さんがいて、もうお下がりばかり着るのはいやだってさ。

4. **Answer** the family resemblance
   彼が君の兄弟だってすぐ分かるよ。だって家族だからそっくりだもの。

5. **Answer** hands-on
   子供たちを新しくできた科学博物館に連れて行こうよ。いろいろ手で触れる展示物があるからすごく喜ぶと思うよ。

6. **Answer** invitations to exhibits
   市長室で仕事をしていて、とても良い事の一つは、町に来る展覧会の招待状がもらえることさ。

7. **Answer** inspired by
   先週家の学校で講演した発明家が言ってたんだけど、彼はエジソンとかベルについて読んだことで刺激を受けたそうだよ。

8. **Answer** an authentic painting
   その絵は美術館の地下に何年間もしまわれていた。ある人がそれは本物のマチスの絵だと気がつくまで。

9. **Answer** have a quick bite
   仕事の帰りに直接シャーリーンの舞踊公演にいくのなら、途中で手早く食べておいた方がいいと思わない？

10. **Answer** frequent my favorite
    好きな近所の映画館が壊される前は、週一度くらい通ってたんだ。

11. **Answer** a second helping
    会社のクリスマスパーティで，全部お代わりしちゃったから，明日から絶対ダイエット始めなくちゃ。

12. **Answer** restaurant review
    新しい客たちをケビンズ・ステーキ・ハウスに連れて行きませんか。レストラン評で著名な料理評論家から素晴らしい評価を受けたんですってよ。

13. **Answer** The outcome of the ballot
    投票結果は今やわが方の候補者に有利なのが明らかだ。選挙本部に行って祝賀会の準備をしなくちゃ。

14. **Answer** apply for a subsidy
    今，市の助成金を申請すれば，本部ビルをソーラー発電に変換して，電力料金を30％節約できる。

15. **Answer** trend-tracking polls
    私の任務は種々の商品動向調査を分析して，それにもとづいて，どんな新製品を開発すべきかを決定することだ。

16. **Answer** copes with
    シュンイチはまだここの仕事を始めて３ヶ月だけど，顧客と折衝するプレッシャーをとてもうまくこなしていると思うよ。

17. **Answer** earned a good reputation
    品質の改良に努力した結果，わが社の製品はビタミン・サプリ業界で良い評価を獲得した。

18. **Answer** succeed in overcoming
    技術部がソフトウエアに関するいくつかの細かい問題点を解決すれば，わが社は史上初の「顔を認識できるロボット」を市場化できるようになる。

19. **Answer** forwarding agent
    月曜日までに米250袋を問屋まで届けなければならない。運送業者が確実に今日中に集荷に来るように手配しなさい。

20. **Answer** launching a new product
    A: わーお！ この素敵な香りは何？
    B: 私たちよ。香水の新製品を売り出すための報道関係お披露目パーティから帰って来たところなの。

Power Builder Chart

/20	/20	/20	/20	/20	/20	/20	/20	/20	/20

黒猫トントンのちょっとブレイク 6

How to Get Married
結婚するには？

トントン： **Big news! Big news! My childhood buddy tabby, Kotaro, is getting married.** 僕の幼なじみのトラ猫コタローが結婚するんだって。

オーガ： **What? Who in the world volunteered to marry a skinny nervous geek like Kotaro?** ヘー，あのやせっぽちの気の弱い変わり者と結婚する物好きはだれなんだ？ 彼が去年の春から **persistently wooing** しつこく言い寄ってた，例の **calico cat Zelda** 三毛猫ゼルダかな？

トントン： **ピンポーン**。

オーガ： まあとにかく **Congratulation is in order!** おめでとうということだ！ **I wonder what kind of kittens they are going to have, mix-breed tabby and calico kittens?** 子供はどんなのが生まれるだろうな。トラ猫と三毛猫だからなー。しかし，猫は一度に **sextuplets** 6匹も生むからなー。**feline population explosion** 猫の人口爆発が心配だな。ウーン。またその節は **contraceptive measures** 避妊相談にのろうと言って置きなさい。

と言うわけで，**Kotaro** のおめでたニュースにちなんで，今日のオーガの **theme** は外国で結婚するときについて。ここでは特に米国の例に絞ってみよう。おっと，それでは，英語の **one point:**

get married と is married は違う

「結婚する」と言うときは action verb「動作またはポイントの動詞」で **get married**「結婚している」は state verb「状態の動詞」で **be married/have been married** と違う表現をとることに気をつけよう。

「**Emma** と **Jun** は昨年結婚した」は
  Emma and Jun got married last year.
「**Emma** と **Jun** は結婚している」は **Emma and Jun are married.**
「**Emma** と **Jun** は結婚して 10 年になる」は
  Emma and Jun have been married for ten years.

米国で結婚するにはまず **marriage license**「結婚許可証」が必要だ。次の **paragraphs** の **keyword** を **check off** しながら速読し，**How to get a marriage license and then marriage certificate** 結婚許可証のとりかたを学ぼう。

※結婚許可証 marriage license と結婚証明書 marriage certificate の違いに注意。

How to Get Married in America

Born and raised in America, and you might find someone you like very much. And then, naturally you will fall in love with this person, get engaged, and finally set a date for the wedding. Then, all hell breaks loose! Ooops, excuse me. I mean you will enjoy going through all the heavenly premarital protocol.

Now, you have to get a marriage license. In order to get a marriage license, the first thing you should do is to get a birth certificate at the city hall. This is similar to the Japanese family register. However, unlike the family register, the birth certificate is based on only your birth status with your father's name and your mother's maiden name on the top.

> Also, in order to issue a marriage license, every state requires blood tests for syphilis. You may take one at any general practitioner and the result will be out in a few days.
>
> Now, take your birth certificate and the result of your blood test to the city hall or the courthouse, and then you can obtain a marriage license.
>
> If it is a religious ceremony, a clergyman, and if a civil one, the justice of the peace, performs the ceremony. Then the bride, groom, and clergyman or the justice of the peace sign the marriage certificate. This is what makes the marriage legal. Congratulations! You and your spouse have now become brand-new newlyweds!

次に結婚証明書の取り方をステップ順に **First, Next, After that, Then, Finally** までキーワードを使って並べてみよう。

First,

Next,

After that,

Then,

Finally,

本文訳

米国に生まれ育って，誰かいい人に会う，当然この人と恋に落ちる，婚約して結婚式の日にちを決める。そして,地獄の毎日が始まるんだ！ おっと,失礼。楽しい結婚前の色々な手続きを楽しむことになるんだ。

そこで，君は結婚許可証なるものをとらなければらない。結婚許可証をえるのに，まず最初にすることは，市役所で出生証明書をとること。これは日本での戸籍謄本にあたる。しかし，戸籍謄本と違い，出世証明書は本人の出生についてと，父親の名前と母親の婚前の名前のみが記録されている。

また結婚許可証をとるためには，どの州でも，梅毒のための血液検査を必要とする。どこの内科医院でも受けられるし，結果は数日中にでる。

では，出生証明書と血液検査の結果を市役所または，裁判所にもっていき，結婚許可証を得ることができる。

宗教的な結婚式なら牧師に，民事的な結婚式なら治安判事に結婚許可証を提示する。

そして，花婿，花嫁と牧師または治安判事が結婚証明書に署名する。これで結婚が法的に成立した。おめでとう！ 君と君の配偶者はほやほやの新婚さんだ。

解答

First, get a birth certificate at the city hall.

Next, take a blood test.

After that, take them to the city hall or courthouse and get a marriage **license**.

Then, the bride and groom take the marriage **license** to either a clergyman or justice of the peace.

Finally, the bride and groom and the clergyman or justice of the peace sign the marriage **certificate**.

Unit 7-1

ショッピング

左の欄から言葉を選んで......を完成しよう!

301 あちこち比較して買い物をする
do c........n shopping

302 ジーンズは皆手頃な値段で売られている。
All jeans are sold at re.......e prices.

303 カタログを請求する
send for a br.....e

304 最新型の携帯を現在販売中です
the newest model m....e currently av......e

305 商品の取り替えに関するきまり
a re........t policy

annual
available
brochure
comparison
economy
line
mobile
reasonable
replacement
rummage
specialist
spree
stand
support

306 次から次へと買い物のはしごをする
go on a shopping sp..e

307 レジの列に並ぶ
st..d in l..e at the cashier

308 シリアルのお徳用袋を買う
buy an ec....y-size bag of cereal

309 顧客担当の専門相談員
a customer-su....t sp.......t

310 年に一度の一掃セール
an an...l ru....e sale

一回で満点を取るより,何回もやってようやく満点を取る人の方が最後は勝つんだよ。その方が頭の中の memory mechanism(記憶装置)にしっかり残るからだ。

Unit 7-1

フレーズ 301 個目から 310 個目までの答えをチェックしよう！ CD38

301 do comparison shopping
[kəmpǽrisn]

302 All jeans are sold at reasonable prices.
[ríːznəbl]

303 send for a brochure
[brouʃúəsr]

304 the newest model mobile currently available
[kə́ːrəntli]

305 a replacement policy
[ripléismənt]

306 go on a shopping spree
[spríː]

307 stand in line at the cashier*
[kæʃíər]
*chashier は i の上にアクセント。間違えると通じないから注意。

308 buy an economy-size bag of cereal
[síəriəl]

309 a customer-support specialist
[spéʃəlist]

310 an annual rummage sale
[rʌ́midʒ]

点数チェック

/10 /10 /10 /10 /10 /10 /10 /10 /10 /10

Unit 7-2

天候・災害

左の欄から言葉を選んで......を完成しよう！

311 お天気キャスター
a weather fo.......r

312 稲妻をともなった激しい雷雨
fierce th.........m with li......g

313 土石流による死傷者
ca......es caused by the mu.....e

314 蒸し暑い日
a hot and mu..y day

315 放射能の蓄積
ra......n buildup

316 干ばつにやられた地帯
dr....t-st.....n area

317 適度な湿度を保つ
keep ad.....e hu.....y

318 避難口
an ev.......n exit

319 震源地
the ep......r of the earthquake

320 震度8の地震
an earthquake with a seismic in......y of 8

adequate
casualties
drought
epicenter
evacuation
forecaster
humidity
intensity
lightning
mudslide
muggy
radiation
stricken
thunderstorm

一回で満点を取るより，何回もやってようやく満点を取る人の方が最後は勝つんだよ。
その方が頭の中の memory mechanism（記憶装置）にしっかり残るからだ。

Unit 7-2

フレーズ 311 個目から 320 個目までの答えをチェックしよう！　CD39

311 a weather forecaster
[fɔ́:kæstər]

312 fierce thunderstorm with lightning
[fíərs]　[θʌ́ndərstɔ́:rm]

313 casualties caused by the mudslide
[kǽʒuəlti:z]

314 a hot and muggy day
[mʌ́gi]

315 radiation buildup
[rèidiéiʃən]

316 drought*-stricken area
[dráut] *発音注意。ドラフトビール draught beer の [drá:ft] と間違えないように。

317 keep adequate humidity
[ǽdikwət]

318 an evacuation exit
[ivækjuéiʃən]　[égzit]

319 the epicenter of an earthquake
[épisentər]

320 an earthquake with a seismic intensity of 8
[sáizmik]

点数チェック
/10 /10 /10 /10 /10 /10 /10 /10 /10 /10

Unit 7-3

スポーツとゲーム

左の欄から言葉を選んで……を完成しよう！

321 体操競技
a gy.......s com.......n

322 全く素晴らしい成果
totally aw....e achievement

323 膠着状態を打ち破るホームラン
a homerun to break the st......e

324 オリンピック級の選手
an Olympic-ca....r athlete

325 接戦で闘う
fight a ti..t ba...e

326 運動神経に優れている
at.........y inclined

327 逆転勝ちする
win a come-from-be...d vi....y

328 会員になる資格がある
el.....e for membership

329 ハワイマラソンの参加申込書を出す
su...t an en..y form for the Hawaii Marathon

330 世界記録をうちたてる
es......h a world record

athletically
awesome
battle
behind
caliber
competition
eligible
entry
establish
gymnastics
stalemate
submit
tight
victory

一回で満点を取るより，何回もやってようやく満点を取る人の方が最後は勝つんだよ。
その方が頭の中のmemory mechanism（記憶装置）にしっかり残るからだ。

Unit 7-3

フレーズ 321 個目から 330 個目までの答えをチェックしよう！ CD40

321 a gymnastics competition
[dʒimnǽstiks]

322 totally awesome achievement
[ɔ́:səm]

323 a homerun to break the stalemate
[stéilmèit]

324 Olympic-caliber athlete
[kǽləbər]

325 fight a tight battle

326 athletically inclined
[æθlétikəli]

327 win a come-from-behind victory
[víktəri]

328 eligible for membership
[élidʒəbl]

329 submit an entry form for the Hawaii Marathon
[éntri]

330 establish a world record
[istǽbliʃ]

点数チェック

Unit 7-4

農業・農産物

左の欄から言葉を選んで...... を完成しよう！

agricultural
cultivate
dairy
disease
eliminate
fertile
livestock
manure
organically
perennial
pesticide
poisoning
produce
yields

331 農産物
ag.........l pr....e

332 畜産業
li......k farming

333 多年草
pe.....al plants

334 年間の穀物収穫量
annual crop yi..ds

335 乳製品
da..y products

336 狂牛病を絶滅させる
el......e mad cow di....e

337 リンゴ栽培に牛糞肥料を使う
use cow ma...e for growing apples

338 有機肥料で育てられたナス
or.......ly grown eggplants

339 肥沃な土壌を作る
cu......e fe....e soil

340 農業従事者を農薬中毒から守る
protect farm workers from pe......e po......g

一回で満点を取るより，何回もやってようやく満点を取る人の方が最後は勝つんだよ。その方が頭の中の memory mechanism（記憶装置）にしっかり残るからだ。

Unit 7-4

フレーズ 331 個目から 340 個目までの答えをチェックしよう！ CD41

331 **agricultural produce**
[ægrikʌ́ltʃərəl]

332 **livestock farming**
[láivstɑ́k]

333 **perennial plants**
[pəréniəl] *annual plants 一年生の植物

334 **annual crop yields**
[jíːlz]

335 **dairy products**
[déəri]

336 **eliminate mad cow disease**
[ilímənèit]

337 **use cow manure for growing apples**
[mənjúər]

338 **organically grown eggplants**
[ɔːrgǽnikəliː]

339 **cultivate fertile soil**
[fɔ́ːrtl] *発音注意。「ファーティル」

340 **protect farm workers from pesticide poisoning**
[péstəsàid]

点数チェック

/10 /10 /10 /10 /10 /10 /10 /10 /10 /10

Unit 7-5

コンピューターとネット (1)

左の欄から言葉を選んで......を完成しよう！

341 自分のフェイスブックページを作る
cu......e one's Facebook page

342 プリンターなどのコンピューター周辺機器
printers and other computer pe.......ls

343 電子工業界の大企業
el.......cs gi..t

344 各部屋にワイファイ設備の用意あり
in-room Wi-Fi pr.....d

345 ブログを更新する
up...e a blog

346 講座登録をEメールで申し込む
email in a co...e re.........n

347 顧客リストは第三者には公表できない。
The customer list is not di......d to third pa...es.

348 最先端のテクノロジー
cu....g-e..e technology

349 社内用ネットワーク設備を改良する
up....e the in.....t in our office

350 このアイコンは音量を示します。
This icon in......s the volume.

course
customize
cutting
disclosed
edge
electronics
giant
indicates
intranet
parties
peripherals
provided
registration
update
upgrade

一回で満点を取るより，何回もやってようやく満点を取る人の方が最後は勝つんだよ。
その方が頭の中の memory mechanism（記憶装置）にしっかり残るからだ。

Unit 7-5

フレーズ 341 個目から 350 個目までの答えをチェックしよう！ CD42

341 customize one's Facebook page
[kʌ́stəmàiz]

342 printers and other computer peripherals
[pərífərəlz]

343 electronics giant
[ilektrániks]

344 in-room Wi-Fi provided
[prəváidid]

345 update a blog*
*blog は web と log をつないだもの。

346 email in* a course registration
*email in で「email で送りこむ」という idiom。 [rèdʒistréiʃən]

347 The customer list is not disclosed to third parties.
[disklóuzd]

348 cutting-edge technology
[teknálədʒi]

349 upgrade the intranet in our office

350 This icon indicates the volume.
[áikɑn]

点数チェック

Review Quiz for Unit 7

> ではここまで演習してきたら，君の記憶はかんぺきなはず。そこで Unit のおさらいをしよう。テキストを見ずに文の ……………… を埋められるかな？ 何度でも復習できるように，書き込みはせずにやってみよう。
>
> ここにある文は，実際の「TOIEC Part 5 短文穴埋め問題」のものとほぼ同じ長さになっている。だからこの REVIEW QUIZ も TOEIC と同じペースで，1問を 15 秒以内で答えるようにしよう。
>
> 1回目は絶対に辞書を使わないこと！ キーワードを拾って記憶で勝負！
>
> 必要に応じて，語形を変えることを忘れないように。
> タイマーを5分に設定して，READY SET GO！
>
> CD43

1. A: I need to buy a new washing machine, but I'm not sure which one to get.
   B: Well, you should always do some ……………… first to make sure you get the best quality for the price.

2. If you are going to buy cat food, I recommend the new supermarket on Third Street. They have very ……………… .

3. I'm sorry, but we won't be able to repair the copier for another few days.. The parts you need are not ……………… .

4. Look at this! This suitcase is brand new and the handle is already broken. Thank goodness the manufacturer has ……………… .

5. A: How was your company picnic?
   B: Don't you remember? We had ……………… on Saturday morning and had to cancel our plans.

6. The U.N. has made it a top priority to eliminate all ……………… land mines within two years.

7. A: Vegetables are awfully expensive this summer, aren't they?
   B: They sure are. It's because the farming areas have been ……………… .

8. The .... was about 600 miles off the coast of Chile at a depth of approximately 50 miles.

9. I'm going to go home early tonight and watch the Olympics on TV. Tonight is the .... , my favorite part.

10. Look at George swimming like a frog! He won the last national competition and certainly is .... swimmer.

11. I've started jogging recently. For people like me who are not .... , it's the perfect sport.

12. For me the Indians' .... against the Mariners when they were down by six runs was the most exciting baseball game I've ever seen.

13. I just inherited some land from my Uncle Rick. It's not so good for growing crops, but I've always wanted to try .... with lots of cows.

14. The .... were low this year, but I'm new at farming. I'll have a better harvest next year.

15. I'm afraid we're going to have to inspect all of your cattle, Mr. Baker. You understand how important it is to ....

16. My wife and I decided to change our family's eating habits. Now everything we eat at our house is .... , and not only do our meals taste much better, but they are healthier as well.

17. I told our children not to play in our neighbor's back yard. He uses lots of chemicals in his garden and I'm worried about ....

18. A: You certainly were in that meeting for a long time.
    B: Tell me about it! The Accounting Section and the Purchasing Section were arguing over how to .... on the computers.

19. You have to be more careful with computer security. This kind of information should never be .... anyone outside the company.

Review Quiz for Unit 7

131

20. I'm looking forward to the Electronics Show in Las Vegas next week. They are going to be exhibiting some .... smart TVs that I'm really interested in checking out.

1. **Answer** comparison shopping
   A: 新しい洗濯機を買いたいんだけど，どれを買ったらいいのか分からないんだ。
   B: まず色々比較してから買い物すべきだよ。そしてその値段のなかで一番良い物を買うようにするべきよ。

2. **Answer** reasonable prices
   猫の餌を買うのなら，三番街の新しいスーパーがいいよ。値段が安いから。

3. **Answer** currently available
   すみませんが，コピー機の修繕には2，3日お待ち頂くことになります。スペアのパーツが現在品切れでして。

4. **Answer** a replacement policy
   見てよ！このスーツケース真っさらなのにハンドルが壊れてるの。製造会社に取り替え保証制度があって良かったけどね。

5. **Answer** the fierce thunderstorm
   A: テニスの試合はどうだった？
   B: 覚えてないの？ 土曜日はものすごい雷雨だったでしょう。だから予定はキャンセルになったの。

6. **Answer** casualties caused by
   国連は二年以内にすべての地雷被害を除くことを最優先事項とした。

7. **Answer** drought stricken
   A: 今年は野菜がやけに高いと思わない？
   B: 全くだよ。農業地帯が干ばつ被害に遭っているからなんだよね。

8. **Answer** epicenter of the earthquake
   震源地はチリ沖600マイル，深度ほぼ50マイルです。

9. **Answer** gymnastics competition
   今日は早く帰って，テレビでオリンピックを見るつもり。今夜は体操競技で，私の好きな種目なんだ。

10. **Answer** an Olympic-caliber
    見ろよ，ジョージは蛙みたいに泳いでる。彼は最近の国内競技にも優勝したし，絶対オリンピック級のスイマーだ。

11. **Answer** athletically inclined
最近ジョギングを始めたの。私のように運動神経のない人にとっては，最適のスポーツだから。

12. **Answer** come-from-behind victory
私が見たのでは，対マリナーズ戦でインディアンズが6点も負けていたのにそこから逆転勝ちしたときが，私が見た中で一番興奮した試合だったな。

13. **Answer** livestock farming
リック伯父さんから，土地を相続したところなんだ。あまり作物には向かないけど，でもずっと牛をたくさん飼って畜産をやってみたいと思っていたんだ。

14. **Answer** crop yields
今年の収穫量は良くなかったけど，でも私はまだ農業は新米だからね。来年はもっと良い収穫にするつもりだ。

15. **Answer** eliminate mad cow disease
ベーカーさん，お宅の牛を全部検査しなければなりません。狂牛病根絶の重要さはおわかり頂けますよね。

16. **Answer** organically grown
妻と私は家族全員の食習慣を変えようと決めたんです。今わが家で食べているのは全て有機栽培のもので，だからずっと美味しいし，健康にもいいですよ。

17. **Answer** pesticide poisoning
子供たちに，隣家の裏庭で遊ばないように言った。彼らは大量の化学薬品を庭に使用するから，農薬中毒が心配だから。

18. **Answer** allocate memory
A: 随分長く会議していたんだね。
B: 全くよ。会計課と購買課がコンピューターのメモリーの割り当てでうばいあいになったのよ。

19. **Answer** disclosed to
もっとコンピューターセキュリティについて，注意しなければいけないよ。この情報は絶対に会社の外部に漏れてはならないんだ。

20. **Answer** cutting-edge
ラスベガスでの来週の電子機器見本市に期待してるんだ。最先端の多機能テレビが展示される予定だから，色々と検討しようと思っているんだ。

Power Builder Chart

/20	/20	/20	/20	/20	/20	/20	/20	/20	/20

黒猫トントンのちょっとブレイク 7

Speed Reading
速読講座　Scanning - Part 1

今日は黒猫トントンはお休み。オーガは人間用クラスを主宰する。

TOEIC Part 7 で一番必要なのは、質問に対する答えをいち早く本文から見つけるために scanning すること。だから今日は、scanning の練習をしてみよう。

Step by step, 次のような skill を身につければ、成功間違いなしよ。制限時間は正確に守ろう！

STEP 1　タイマーとペンシルを用意。

STEP 2　タイマーを1分に設定。

STEP 3　次の文中に "down" という言葉を見つけたらすぐに check off（／）しよう。ここでは、文の意味などは考えなくてもよいから、機械的に "down" という語に slash mark（／）をつけること。

例：Population of this village is a little over 5,000.

READY? GO!

STEP 4　ベルが鳴ったらヤメー！　まだ終わっていなくてもヤメー！

A Versatile Little Word: "Down"

Let's start with a little story.

It was a cold day, and so Edward put on his new down jacket. It was a bargain. It had been on sale in a local shop, marked down by 50 percent. Knowing it was time for a walk, his dog Pally started to jump around. "Down, Pally!" he ordered her as he fastened the leash to her collar. He just had time to take her for a walk on the downs near his house before his wife arrived home. She was planning to take the 3:00 p.m. train down from London. After coming back from the walk, he was going to drive down the hill to the station to pick up his wife at 3:45. He remembered the time. He was usually quite forgetful, so his wife had made him write it down. On the drive to the station, he was planning to listen to his favorite podcast, which he had earlier downloaded. After getting back from the station, he was looking forward to downing a whisky and soda before dinner.

STEP 5　パラグラフの終わりまで行けたかな。check off（/）した"down"の数を数えよう。速読に慣れれば，探している言葉が自然に目に飛び込んでくるようになるから，この程度の長さのパラグラフは 20 秒程度でこなせるようになる。

"down" はいくつあったかな？

STEP 6　では，最後にそれぞれの"down"の意味を考えながら，文を楽しもう。分からない言葉は辞書を引いても良いよ。

正解と訳　down の数：10 個

A Versatile Little Word: "Down"

Let's start with a little story.

It was a cold day, and so Edward put on his new down jacket. It was a bargain. It had been on sale in a local shop, marked down by 50 percent. Knowing it was time for a walk, his dog Pally started to jump around. "Down, Pally!"
Edward ordered her as he fastened the leash to her collar. He just had time to take her for a walk on the downs near his house before his wife arrived home. She was planning to take the 3:00 p.m. train down from London. After coming back from the walk, Edward was going to drive down the hill to the station to pick up his wife at 3:45. He remembered the time. He was usually quite forgetful, so his wife had made him write it down. On the drive to the station, he usually listens to his favorite podcast, which he had earlier downloaded. Then, after getting back from the station, he was looking forward to downing a whisky and soda before dinner.

本文訳

大きく役立つ小さな言葉 "Down"

小さな物語を始めよう。それはとても寒い日だったので，エドワードは新しいダウンジャケットを着こんだ。バーゲンで買ったんだ。近くの店でセールになっていて，50％オフになっていたんだ。散歩の時間だというのが分かって，犬のポリーは飛び跳ねている。「ポリー，おとなしくしろ！」エドワードは犬の首に紐を巻きながら命令した。妻が帰宅する前だから，そこの丘まで散歩する時間しかない。彼女はロンドンから3時の電車で帰るはず。だか，エドワードは散歩がすんだら，妻を3時45分に丘を下って迎えにいかねばならない。時間は覚えているんだ。彼は忘れっぽいから，妻は時間を書き留めるように言ったんだ。駅へ行く道すがら，彼はいつもポッドキャストからダウンロードした好きな番組を聴く。そして駅から帰り，夕食の前にウイスキー アンド ソーダを一杯やるんだ。

Unit 8-1

通信・電話

左の欄から言葉を選んで……を完成しよう！

351	未払いの電話料金
	an ou……g telephone bill

352	自分宛の留守電を聞く
	listen to one's vo..e mail

353	電話番号案内で番号を聞く
	ask the number at di……y as……e

354	話し中のシグナル
	get a b..y si..l

assistance
busy
communication
direct
directory
emergency
messaging
outstanding
overnight
parcel
recipient
signal
snail
tree
voice

355	電話連絡網
	telephone co……….n t..e

356	（電話の）受信者
	the re……t of a call

357	国際直通ダイアルコード
	an international di...t-dialing code

358	災害用伝言ダイアル
	an em……y me……g service

359	普通郵便で手紙を送る
	send a letter by sn..l mail

360	翌日配達便で小包を送る
	send a pa...l by ov……t mail

一回で満点を取るより，何回もやってようやく満点を取る人の方が最後は勝つんだよ。その方が頭の中の memory mechanism（記憶装置）にしっかり残るからだ。

Unit 8-1

フレーズ 351 個目から 360 個目までの答えをチェックしよう！ 　CD44

351 an outstanding telephone bill
[áutstændiŋ]

352 listen to one's voice mail

353 ask the number at directory assistance
[diréktəri]

354 get a busy signal

355 telephone communication tree
[kəmjùːnəkéiʃən]

356 the recipient of a call
[risípiənt]

357 an international direct-dialing code
[dirékt]

358 an emergency messaging service
[mésidʒiŋ]

359 send a letter by snail mail*
[snéil]
*snail mail は会話的表現。普通郵便の正式名は surface mail。

360 send a parcel by overnight mail
[páːrsəl]

点数チェック

Unit 8-2

教育・学校

左の欄から言葉を選んで……を完成しよう！

361 期末レポートの提出期限を守る
meet the de.....e for the t..m paper

362 人類学を専攻する
ma..r in an.........y

363 美術を副専攻する
mi..r in fine arts

364 化学で理学士号を得る
earn a ba.....r of science de...e in chemistry

365 （大学の）卒業式
a co.........t ceremony

366 社会人教育プログラム
co.......g education program

367 大学在籍者数
college en.......t

368 公開講座
an ex......n program

369 課外活動
ex...........ar ac......es

370 奨学金を与えられる
gr....d a scholarship

activities
anthropology
bachelor
commencement
continuing
deadline
degree
enrollment
extension
extracurricular
granted
major
minor
term

一回で満点を取るより、何回もやってようやく満点を取る人の方が最後は勝つんだよ。その方が頭の中の memory mechanism（記憶装置）にしっかり残るからだ。

Unit 8-2

フレーズ 361 個目から 370 個目までの答えをチェックしよう！ CD45

361 **meet the deadline for the term paper**
[dédlain]

362 **major* in anthropology**
[méidʒər]   [æ̀nθrəpάlədʒi]
*発音注意。「メジャー」ではなく、「メイジャー」

363 **minor in fine arts**
[máinə(r)]

364 **earn a bachelor of science degree in chemistry**
[bǽtʃələr]

365 **a commencement ceremony**
[kəménsmənt]
*commencement は「社会へのデビュー」という意味で、高校・大学の卒業式に使われる。

366 **continuing education program**
[kəntínjuːíŋ]

367 **college enrollment**
[inróulmənt]

368 **an extension program**
[iksténʃən]

369 **extracurricular activities**
[èkstrəkəríkjulər]

370 **granted a scholarship**
[skάlərʃip]

点数チェック

Unit 8-3
食物とクッキング

左の欄から言葉を選んで......を完成しよう！

371 一ヶ月分の食料品費
a monthly gr....y bill

372 シロップを加えゆっくりまぜる。
Add syrup and s..r slowly.

373 天ぷらの生地を作る。
Mix the ba...r for tempura.

374 自然農法の材料だけを使う
use only natural in.......ts

375 炭火で肉を焙り焼きする
br..l meat on ch.....l

376 独創的な料理をコンテストに送って下さい。
Send in cr.....e re...es for the contest.

377 ケーキのデコレーションとパイの詰め物
cake fr.....g and pie fi....g

378 美味しい料理を楽しむ
enjoy go....t dishes

379 コーヒーの良い香り
the de.......l ar..a of coffee

380 弱火でとろとろ煮えているシチュー
stew si......g on a low heat

aroma
batter
broil
charcoal
creative
delightful
filling
frosting
gourmet
grocery
ingredients
recipes
simmering
stir

一回で満点を取るより、何回もやってようやく満点を取る人の方が最後は勝つんだよ。その方が頭の中の memory mechanism（記憶装置）にしっかり残るからだ。

Unit 8-3

フレーズ 371 個目から 380 個目までの答えをチェックしよう！ CD46

371 **a monthly grocery bill**
[gróusəri]

372 **Add syrup and stir slowly.**
[stə́:r]

373 **Mix the batter for tempura.**
[bǽtə]

374 **use only natural ingredients**
[ingrí:diənts]

375 **broil meat on charcoal**
[brɔ́il]

376 **Send in creative recipes for the contest.**
[résəpi:z]

377 **cake frosting and pie filling**
[frɔ́:stiŋ]

378 **enjoy gourmet dishes**
[guərméi]

379 **the delightful aroma of coffee**
[diláitfəl]

380 **stew simmering on a low heat**
[stjú:] [síməriŋ]

点数チェック

/10 /10 /10 /10 /10 /10 /10 /10 /10 /10

Unit 8-4
製造・工場

左の欄から言葉を選んで......を完成しよう！

381 製造業
the ma..........g industry

382 防護服を着る
put on pr.......e clothing

383 工場長
a plant fo....n

384 全面的操業に入る
go into full-scale op......n

385 自動化された組み立てライン
an au......d assembly facility

386 工場直営店
a fa....y-outlet store

387 設計図を作成する
d..w up a bl......t

388 集配業務を始める
set up a de.....y and co.......n service

389 人件費を節約する
ec.....e on labor costs

390 損失を賠償する
co.......e for the l..s

automated
blueprint
collection
compensate
delivery
draw
economize
factory
foreman
loss
manufacturing
operation
protective

一回で満点を取るより，何回もやってようやく満点を取る人の方が最後は勝つんだよ。その方が頭の中の memory mechanism（記憶装置）にしっかり残るからだ。

Unit 8-4

フレーズ 381 個目から 390 個目までの答えをチェックしよう！　CD47

381 the manufacturing industry
[mæ̀njufǽktʃəríŋ]

382 put on protective clothing
[prətéktiv]　　　[klóuðiŋ]

383 a plant foreman
[fɔ́ːrmən]

384 go into full-scale operation
[àpəréiʃən]

385 an automated assembly facility
[ɔ́ːtəmèitid]　　　　　　[fəsíləti]

386 a factory-outlet store
[fǽktəri]

387 draw up a blueprint
[blúːprint]

388 set up a delivery and collection service
[dilívəri]

389 economize on labor costs
[ikánəmàiz]

390 compensate for the loss
[kámpənsèit]

点数チェック

Unit 8-5

コンピューターとネット (2)

左の欄から言葉を選んで……を完成しよう！

391 コンピューター翻訳ソフト
computer-ai..d tr........n software

392 「フェイスブック」は社交のための連絡網ソフト。
Facebook is a kind of so...l-ne......g service.

393 目立つ見出し広告のデザイン
eye-ca.....g layout of a ba...r advertisement

394 最新型のノートパソコン
a st..e-of-the-art laptop

395 電子マネーによる決済
pay with di....l cash

396 ネット関連の複合大企業
internet co.........e

397 （コンピューター内の）記憶域を割り当てる
al.....e memory on the computer

398 侵入防止ソフト
ha...r-pr..f software

399 （ドアなどの）指紋読み取り器
a fi........t reader

400 情報技術の進歩
ad........ts in information technology (IT)

advancements
aided
allocate
banner
catching
conglomerate
digital
fingerprint
hacker
networking
proof
social
state
translation

一回で満点を取るより、何回もやってようやく満点を取る人の方が最後は勝つんだよ。その方が頭の中の memory mechanism（記憶装置）にしっかり残るからだ。

Unit 8-5

フレーズ 391 個目から 400 個目までの答えをチェックしよう！ CD48

391 computer-aided translation software
[trænsléiʃən]

392 Facebook is a kind of social-networking service.*
*SNS ... social-networking service　社交用ネットワークをインターネット上でつくるサービス事業のことで，日本では mixi, GREE, Mobage, Ameba, 世界では Facebook, Myspace, LinkedIn などがある。

393 eye-catching layout of a banner advertisement
[bǽnər]

394 a state-of-the-art laptop

395 pay with digital* cash
[dídʒətl]
*digital ⇔反対語 analog は目で数量を見られるもの。

396 internet conglomerate
[kənglάmərət]

397 allocate memory on the computer
[ǽləkèit]

398 hacker-proof software

399 a fingerprint reader

400 advancements in information technology (IT)
[ædvǽnsmənts]

点数チェック

| /10 | /10 | /10 | /10 | /10 | /10 | /10 | /10 | /10 | /10 |

Review Quiz for Unit 8　147

ではここまで演習してきたら，君の記憶はかんぺきなはず。そこでUnitのおさらいをしよう。テキストを見ずに文の............を埋められるかな？何度でも復習できるように，書き込みはせずにやってみよう。

ここにある文は，実際の「TOIEC Part 5 短文穴埋め問題」のものとほぼ同じ長さになっている。だからこのREVIEW QUIZもTOEICと同じペースで，1問を15秒以内で答えるようにしよう。

1回目は絶対に辞書を使わないこと！キーワードを拾って記憶で勝負！

必要に応じて，語形を変えることを忘れないように。
タイマーを5分に設定して，READY SET GO！　　CD49

1. I'm very sorry, sir, but until your .... is paid, we will not be able to restore your service.

2. A: I need to make reservations at Stavini's, the Italian restaurant. Do you happen to know their telephone number?
   B: No, but you could call ....

3. Recently, criminal gangs have been telephoning people and pretending to collect donations for victims of the earthquake. If you are .... like that, do not give out your credit-card information over the telephone.

4. I've been having trouble with my server again. You'd better send the documents to me by ....

5. I think the schedule is too tight. The Production Manager almost had a heart attack trying to .... the last time.

6. The second candidate we interviewed might be right for the internship. We need someone for the bookkeeping section, and that candidate is .... accounting at college.

7. I'm afraid the earthquake did so much damage to the school auditorium that we are going to have to hold our .... in a rental space.

8. A: Hey, I hear you joined the mountain-climbing club.
   B: I sure did. I think adding some .... will look good on my resume when I go job-hunting in the future.

9. Why can't the government do anything about inflation? My .... is going sky-high this month and I can barely make ends meet.

10. Everything is almost ready for the birthday party. I'll .... for the cake, so could you grease the baking pan?

11. Since I started to use only .... in my cooking, I do feel much healthier, but at the same time my food bill is much higher.

12. A: Sniff Sniff. Where is this .... coming from?
    B: Oh, that's the new doughnut shop on the corner. They have 28 different kinds and really good coffee.

13. Jane's dad is taking her to see where he works for Bring-Your-Child-To-Work Day. He's .... at the automobile factory.

14. A: .... of B.B. Brothers just opened at the mall.
    B: Perfect! I need a new suit for my job interview next week.

15. Until the company recovers its financial health, I'm afraid we are going to have to .... certain things like business travel. From now on, it's economy class and business hotels for everyone.

16. If we shift our production overseas, maybe we can .... the unfavorable exchange rate.

17. A: I am trying to decide which .... to join. Do you have any good suggestions?
    B: Some of my friends are on Mysite.com. But, I think ComNex.com has the largest number of subscribers.

18. My computer's just about seen its day. But on my salary, I can't really afford .... right now, so I think I'll look for a used one.

19. The company is changing over to a new system of payment. Starting next month, we'll only .... which means we'll have a lot less paperwork.

Review Quiz for Unit 8 149

20. A: Do you think anyone will ever develop absolutely .... ?
    B: I doubt it. Someone will always figure out how to get in. It's a real cat-and-mouse game.

1. **Answer** outstanding telephone bill
   申し訳ありませんが，お客様の未払い電話請求書のお支払がすむまでは，サービスを再開できません。

2. **Answer** directory assistance
   A: スタビニズ・イタリアンレストランを予約しきゃならないんだ。番号知っている？
   B: いいや，でも番号案内に聞けば。

3. **Answer** the recipient of a call
   最近犯罪グループが，人々に電話して地震の被害者への寄付を募るふりをしています。そのような電話を受信されたら，電話でクレジットカード情報など伝えないようにして下さい。

4. **Answer** snail mail
   またまたサーバーがトラブルを起こしています。書類を郵便で送って下さい。

5. **Answer** meet the deadline
   スケジュールが厳しすぎるよ。先回は製造部長が期限に間に合わせようとして，心臓発作を起こしかけたんだぞ。

6. **Answer** minoring in
   2番目に面接した候補者が実習社員として向いていると思う。社で必要なのは簿記係で，あの候補者は会計学を副専攻しているから。

7. **Answer** commencement ceremony
   地震による体育館の被害が甚大なので，卒業式はどこか借りた場所で行わねばならないでしょう。

8. **Answer** extracurricular activities
   A: 山岳部に入ったんだって？
   B: そうとも,将来の就職のために課外活動を履歴書に入れれば役に立つかと思ってさ。

9. **Answer** grocery bill
   なんで政府はインフレ対策ができないんだ？ うちの今月の食料品費はもう限界をこえた，もうやりくりできないよ。

10. **Answer** mix the batter
    誕生日パーティの準備はほとんど完了だ。私がケーキの生地を作るから，君は焼き皿に油を引いて。

11. Answer natural ingredients
料理に自然の材料だけを使うようになってから、ずっと調子が良いけど、でも同時に食費はずっと高くなったよ。

12. Answer delightful aroma
A: クンクン、この美味しそうな香りはどこから来ているのかな？
B: ああ、角の新しいドーナッツショップよ。18種類もあってコーヒーもすごく美味しいんだよ。

13. Answer a plant foreman
ジェーンのパパは「子供を連れて仕事に行く日」に職場を見せに彼女を連れて行くんだって。彼は自動車工場の工場長なんだぜ。

14. Answer A factory-outlet store
A: B.B.Brothers の工場直営アウトレットがモールで開店したよ。
B: ちょうどいい！ 来週の面接のためにスーツが要るんだ。

15. Answer economize on
わが社の財政が立ち直るまで、出張費などを節約しなければならない。これからは、全員エコノミークラス席でビジネスホテル宿泊とする。

16. Answer compensate for
海外に生産拠点を移せば、不利な為替レートを補うことが出来るかもしれない。

17. Answer social-networking service
A: どの連絡網ソフトに入ろうかと考え中なんだ。何かお勧めのある？
B: 友だちは何人か Mysite.com に入っているよ。でも、ComNex.com の加入者が一番多いそうだよ。

18. Answer a state-of-the-art laptop
コンピューターがもう寿命みたいなんだけど、私の給料ではぴかぴかの新品は買えないから、中古品を探そうかな。

19. Answer pay with digital cash
社は新しい支払い制に変更する予定です。来月からすべてを電子マネーによる決済にします。それでペーパーワークはぐっと減ることになる。

20. Answer hacker-proof software
A: 絶対的な侵入者防止ソフトを誰か作るだろうか？
B: どうかな。だれかが必ず侵入方法を見つけるから。追いつ追われつの状況だね。

Power Builder Chart

/20	/20	/20	/20	/20	/20	/20	/20	/20	/20

黒猫トントンの ちょっとブレイク 8

Speed Reading
速読講座　Scanning - Part 2

今日も黒猫トントンはお休み。
オーガは TOEIC 演習クラスを主宰する。

TOEIC Part 7 で必要なのは，質問の答えにマッチする key word を出来るだけ早く拾えるようになること。Speed Reading 1 では，質問に対する答えをいち早く本文から見つけるために一つの言葉を拾う scanning skill を練習した。

今回は文中にある「数字」を scanning する練習をしてみよう。TOEIC テスト，Reading Comprehension などに出る問題の一つに，数字の意味を問うものがある。全ての数字を覚えている必要は無いが，質問の答えとなる数字情報をいかに早く見つけるかはとても大切。次に多くの数字を含む paragraph の中から，まず 1) 数字を scanning し，2) その数字の意味を表す keyword を拾う練習をしよう。

各 STEP にしたがっていけば，成功間違いなし。制限時間は正確に守ろうね！

STEP 1　タイマーとペンシルを用意。

STEP 2　タイマーを 30 秒に設定。

STEP 3　文中の数字をみつけたら即，機械的に check off（／）しよう。

例：Population of this village is a little over 5,000.
READY? GO!

Energy Problems and Solutions

There is a lot of talk these days about decreasing energy consumption. But is energy consumption really increasing? It turns out that it is not just increasing—it's skyrocketing. According to the International Energy Agency, the world will need around 60 percent more energy in 2030 than in 2020. Much of this increased demand will come from emerging countries such as China. China consumed 2.2 billion tons of "oil equivalent" in 2009, exceeding the US consumption total of 2.17 billion tons by about four percent. Just 10 years earlier, China consumed just half as much as the United States. But with a population of around 300 million, the United States still uses the most energy per capita of any country in the world. As energy consumption increases, so do prices and pollution. To save money and the planet, something needs to be done.

黒猫トントンのちょっとブレイク

STEP 4 ベルが鳴ったらヤメー！ まだ終わっていなくてもヤメー！
文の終わりまで行けたかな。速読に慣れれば, 情報になる言葉が飛び込んでくるようになるから, この程度の長さの文の **scanning** は10秒程度でこなせるようになる。
数字はいくつあったかな？

STEP 5 次にタイマーを2分に設定して, チェックした数字が意味する言葉を **PARAGRAPH** から見つけてチェック「／」を入れよう。タイマーを1分に設定して **READY? GO!**

例：**Pop/ulation of this village is a little over 5,0̸00.**

STEP 6 ベルが鳴ったらヤメー！ すぐに答えをチェックしよう。

STEP 7 ここで, 心ゆくまで読んで復習しよう。分からない言葉があったら辞書を引いてもいいよ。

STEP 4　正解：8個
60, 2030, 2020, 2.2 billion, 2009, 2.17 billion, 10, 300 million

正解と訳 (数字正解は赤，その数字の意味を表す key word は下線で示しています。)

Energy Problems and Solutions

There is a lot of talk these days about decreasing energy consumption. But is consumption really increasing? It turns out that it is not just increasing—it's skyrocketing. According to the International Energy Agency, the world will need around 60 percent more energy in 2030 than in 2020. Much of this increased demand will come from emerging countries such as China. China consumed 2.2 billion tons of "oil equivalent" in 2009, exceeding the US consumption total of 2.17 billion tons. Just 10 years earlier, China consumed just half as much as the United States. But with a population of around 300 million, the United States still uses the most energy per capita of any country in the world. As energy consumption increases, so do prices and pollution. To save money and the planet, something needs to be done.

本文訳

今日エネルギー消費削減について多くの論議がなされているが，はたして消費は本当に増加しているのだろうか？ 判ったのは，単なる増加ではなくロケットの勢いで激増しているということだ。国際エネルギー協議会によると，2030年代には，世界は2020年代のそれを約60％も上回るエネルギーが必要になるだろうという。需要増加の多くは，たとえば中国のような急成長する国々から発せられている。2009年，中国は22.0億トンの「化石燃料」を消費しており，それは米国の総消費量21.7億トンを4％も上回っている。わずか10年前，中国の消費量は米国のちょうど半分に過ぎなかった。しかし30億の人口をもつ中国より，一人あたりのエネルギー消費量は米国が世界のどの国よりもっとも多い。エネルギー消費が増加するにつれ，価格と汚染も上昇している。経済と地球を守るために，なんらかの手段がとられなければならない。

155

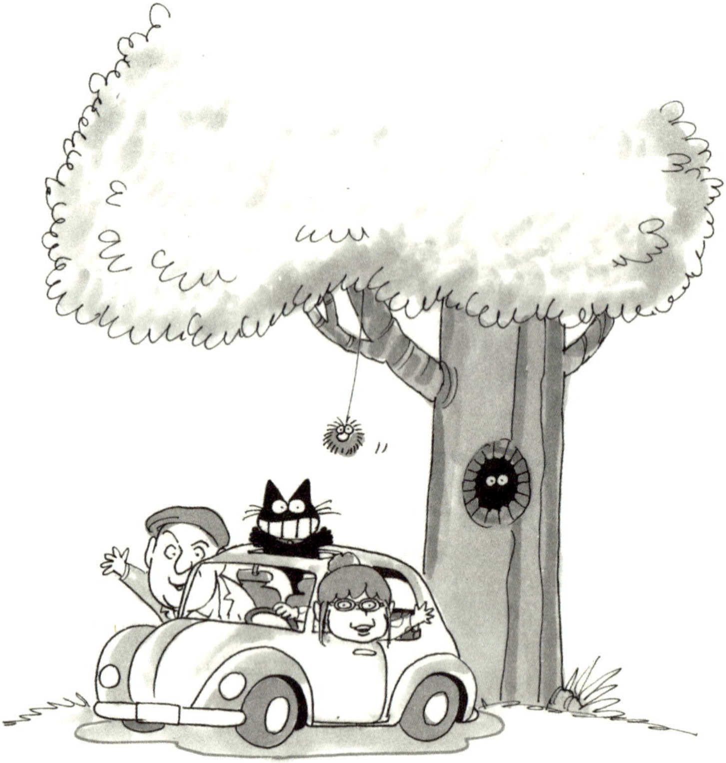

INDEX

※数字は英文の通しナンバー

A

- accept 127
- accommodations 120
- activities 66, 369
- additional 250
- adequate 317
- advance 91
- advancements 400
- adventurous 60
- advertisement 39, 393
- advisor 56
- advisories 27
- affiliate 200
- affiliation 293
- aggravating 203
- aggressive 8
- agile 2
- agricultural 331
- aided 391
- alarm 230
- allocate 397
- allowance 227
- amalgamation 97
- ambulance 183
- amenities 113
- amiable 52
- ankle 189
- anniversary 258
- announcement 266
- annual 310, 334
- anthropology 362
- apologize 26
- appetizer 277
- appliances 173
- appreciative 102
- approach 94
- appropriate 155
- approval 93, 287
- archeology 269
- aroma 379
- arrangements 272
- assigned 144
- assistance 75, 353
- associate 145
- athletically 326
- atmosphere 17
- attend 41
- attention 27
- authentic 270
- authorize 194
- automated 385
- available 304
- average 124
- award 164
- awesome 322
- awkward 153

B

- bachelor 364
- background 267
- ballot 283
- banner 393
- banquet 275
- basal 172
- batter 373
- battle 325
- behavior 153
- behind 327
- birth 251
- birthrate 259
- bite 271
- blackout 215
- blank 151
- blueprint 387
- board 43, 122, 294
- book 111
- break 198, 323
- breakdown 80
- breathe 14
- bribery 289
- brochure 303
- broil 375
- browsing 204
- bulletin 167, 294
- business 145, 191, 248
- busy 354

C

- cabinet 287
- caliber 324
- campaign 40, 281
- cancellation 116
- candidate 121
- capacity 174
- casualties 313
- catching 393
- catering 119, 272
- causes 62
- caution 85
- celebrity 162
- certificate 251
- charcoal 375

- charitable 62
- cheerful 105
- chief 58, 161
- chip 255
- chronic 16
- claim 24
- client 107
- close 248
- collection 68, 388
- columnist 31
- combustible 88
- come 21, 327
- commencement 365
- commentary 34
- communication 355
- commuter 203
- companion 253
- comparison 301
- compensate 390
- competent 51
- competition 321
- complimentary 113
- concerned 154
- concierge 117
- conflict 292
- congestion 228
- conglomerate 396
- consciousness 184
- conserve 211
- considerate 56
- constructive 95
- contact 150
- continental 225
- continuing 366
- cope 290
- corporation 200
- correspondent 36
- count 237
- counter 182
- coupon 73
- courageous 9
- course 346
- coverage 168
- coworkers 51
- creative 376
- crew 183
- crisis 65, 290
- crosswalk 76
- cultivate 339
- curator 264
- customize 341
- cutback 46
- cutting 348

D

- dairy 335
- deadline 361
- deal 248
- declining 259
- degree 364
- delay 26
- delayed 180
- delightful 379
- delinquent 4
- delivery 388
- dental 138, 188
- deny 289
- depressed 190
- descendant 257
- description 42
- destination 28
- determined 108
- development 47, 245
- devoted 9
- diehard 1
- digital 395
- direct 357
- directions 199
- directory 353
- disabled 223
- disappearance 81
- disclosed 347
- disease 336
- disorder 239
- distinguished 246
- distribute 33
- document 296
- dominated 163
- donate 185
- downs 256
- draft 192
- draw 177, 192, 387
- driving 74, 77
- drought 316

E

- easygoing 105
- eating 233, 239
- ecological 83
- economize 389
- economy 308
- edge 348
- edition 38

☐ editor	161	☐ failure	133	☐ global	89
☐ effective	195	☐ fair	41	☐ gourmet	378
☐ electronic	166	☐ fare	73	☐ granted	370
☐ electronics	343	☐ favor	18	☐ green	86
☐ eligible	328	☐ favorite	276	☐ grocery	371
☐ eliminate	336	☐ feeble	13	☐ grudge	160
☐ embarrassing	19	☐ feed	78	☐ gymnastics	321
☐ emergency	230, 358	☐ feedback	242		
☐ eminent	164	☐ fertile	339	**H**	
☐ emitting	178	☐ fill	100, 242		
☐ emotional	67	☐ filled	140	☐ hacker	398
☐ employee	123	☐ filling	377	☐ hail	229
☐ enrollment	367	☐ fingerprint	399	☐ hand	256
☐ entertaining	54	☐ flight	226	☐ handling	250
☐ enthusiast	110	☐ flyers	170	☐ hands	261
☐ entry	329	☐ follow	199, 231	☐ headache	134
☐ epicenter	319	☐ forecaster	311	☐ headquarters	281
☐ epidemic	187	☐ foreman	383	☐ healthcare	131
☐ erratic	233	☐ formally	275	☐ heatstroke	186
☐ establish	249, 330	☐ forwarding	298	☐ helping	279
☐ estimate	98	☐ fossil	217	☐ hike	118
☐ evacuation	318	☐ found	22	☐ historical	267
☐ even	12	☐ freelance	31	☐ homemaker	109
☐ exhibit	262	☐ frequent	25, 276	☐ honking	221
☐ expectant	254	☐ friendly	234	☐ hospitable	17
☐ expenditures	243	☐ frontrunner	108	☐ hospitality	115
☐ expired	78	☐ frosting	377	☐ household	173
☐ extension	368	☐ fuel	143, 217	☐ humidity	317
☐ extinct	87	☐ function	180	☐ hydraulic	218
☐ extracurricular	369	☐ fundraiser	70	☐ hydrogen	216

F   **G**   **I**

| ☐ factors | 240 | ☐ gargle | 202 | ☐ impact | 213 |
| ☐ factory | 386 | ☐ giant | 343 | ☐ income | 124 |

index	232
indicates	350
indulge	156
inefficient	53
influence	74
information	150, 400
informed	273
infrastructure	249
ingredients	374
inquiry	193
inquisitive	59
inspired	265
intake	237
intensity	320
interpreter	61
interrupt	167
intranet	349
invoice	142
issue	37
itinerary	23

J

| journalism | 166 |
| judgment | 152 |

K

| kill | 204 |
| kitchen | 63 |

L

launch	300
laundry	206
lean	2
learner's	79
leftovers	274
license	252
lifeline	64
lightning	312
line	307
livestock	332
loss	390
lost	22
loyal	244
luxurious	114, 225

M

macrobiotic	231
maintain	188, 299
major	362
malignant	135
manufacturing	381
manure	337
margin	299
marriage	252
masculine	55
mass	232
massive	215
masterpiece	265
mean	7
medicine	182
mediocre	241
meltdown	84
messaging	358
minor	363
minute	116, 176
miscellaneous	147
mobile	304
morale	197
motivated	101
mouthwatering	278
mower	207
mudslide	313
muggy	314

N

negotiate	112
networking	392
nomination	286
notice	294
notify	91
nuclear	84
nutritional	240

O

obtain	29
offer	95, 127, 244
online	43, 49
operation	384
organically	338
organization	66
organized	44
orientation	123
outcome	283
outlet	171, 386
outstanding	351
overcoming	295
overnight	360
overtime	126

P

- parcel 360
- participants 10
- particular 117
- parties 347
- paycheck 48
- pedestrian 76
- perennial 333
- period 45, 128
- peripherals 342
- perky 11
- permit 79
- person 8, 44, 104, 109, 162
- persuade 196
- pesticide 340
- photocopier 176
- physical 137
- please 107
- plug 171
- plumbing 179
- point 151
- poisoning 340
- policy 50, 305
- poll 288
- pollen 136
- pollution 82
- postpone 138
- potential 94, 220
- potluck 208
- prescription 140
- primitive 268
- priority 223
- probation 45
- produce 331
- professional 129
- proficient 96
- profit 149, 299
- progressive 282
- promotional 40
- proof 398
- protective 382
- protein 236
- provided 344
- public 297
- publicity 165
- purchase 99

Q

- questionnaire 242
- quick 271

R

- racket 210
- radiation 315
- rain 81
- raise 210
- rash 139
- reasonable 302
- recipes 376
- recipient 356
- reckless 77
- recruits 198
- reduction 235
- references 129
- refugees 69
- registration 346
- regretful 158
- regrettable 159
- relations 297
- release 33
- reliable 32
- relief 14, 64
- replacement 305
- reputation 291
- resemblance 260
- resolve 292
- resources 47, 90
- respond 193
- responsible 44
- revenue 39
- review 280
- reward 244
- rinse 202
- risk 133
- rival 97
- robust 103
- routine 201
- rubbish 205
- rude 4
- ruler 177
- rummage 310
- run 63, 132, 195

S

- safety 249
- sampler 277
- scratch 139
- sculpture 263
- second 15, 279
- sense 157
- sensible 6

☐ sensitive	5	☐ stooped	104	☐ transportation	227
☐ served	21	☐ straight	177	☐ tree	175, 355
☐ shape	238	☐ stricken	316	☐ trend	288
☐ shower	255	☐ submit	49, 329		
☐ shuttle	226	☐ subscribe	35	**U**	
☐ sightseeing	29	☐ subsidy	285		
☐ signal	354	☐ suitable	121	☐ unlimited	220
☐ simmering	380	☐ suite	114	☐ upcoming	266
☐ site	85	☐ superintendent	53	☐ update	345
☐ skeptical	57	☐ supplies	141	☐ upgrade	349
☐ skyrocketing	143	☐ support	66, 309	☐ urgent	100
☐ slump	295	☐ supportive	3		
☐ snail	359	☐ sustainable	90	**V**	
☐ sociable	106	☐ sustaining	214		
☐ social	392			☐ vacuum	209
☐ sore	181	**T**		☐ vehicle	224
☐ sound	152			☐ victims	68
☐ soup	63	☐ tactics	247	☐ victory	327
☐ source	32, 213	☐ talk	20, 157	☐ view	111
☐ specialist	309	☐ tape	92	☐ virtual	169
☐ spits	176	☐ tardiness	16	☐ voice	352
☐ splendid	10	☐ technical	293	☐ voltage	212
☐ spokesperson	284	☐ teller	52		
☐ sprained	189	☐ temperature	132	**W**	
☐ spree	306	☐ tempered	58		
☐ stalemate	323	☐ term	361	☐ warming	89
☐ stalled	72	☐ thermometer	172	☐ wholesaler	148
☐ stand	307	☐ thoughts	15	☐ workweek	130
☐ starting	125	☐ thunderstorm	312		
☐ state	394	☐ tight	325	**Y**	
☐ static	219	☐ tourism	30		
☐ stationery	141	☐ traffic	71, 222	☐ yields	334
☐ stepladder	175	☐ training	128		
☐ stir	372	☐ transferred	146		
☐ stocky	103	☐ translation	391		

執筆協力者
Alan Gleason
Bill Benfield
Terry Browning

TOEIC®テスト攻略 トントンメソッド ＜銅メダルコース Book 1＞

2014年9月17日　1刷

著　者	大賀　リヱ
	デイビッド セイン
イラスト	さとう　有作
装　丁	銀　月　堂
発行者	南　雲　一　範

印刷所	日本ハイコム株式会社
製本所	有限会社松村製本所
発行所	株式会社　南雲堂

東京都新宿区山吹町361番地／〒162-0801
振替口座・00160-0-46863
TEL (03) 3268-2311　FAX (03) 3260-5425
E-mail：nanundo@post.email.ne.jp
URL：http://www.nanun-do.co.jp

乱丁・落丁本はご面倒ですが小社通販係宛ご送付下さい。
送料小社負担にてお取替えいたします。

Printed in Japan　（検印省略）
ISBN978-4-523-25158-3　C0082　＜G-158＞

まだまだ続く、
元祖!! 発信型の単語集!!

英単語ピーナツほど
おいしいものはない

元祖!!

清水かつぞー
著

東大生もみんな読んでいた!?

全国の書店にて ㊙ ㊙ 発売中！

英単語探求の道!!
シリーズ累計100万部のベストセラー!

金 Going for the Gold
メダルコース　【改訂新版】フルカラー
ISBN978-4-523-25155-2 C7082

銀 Going for the Silver
メダルコース　【改訂新版】フルカラー
ISBN978-4-523-25154-5 C7082

銅 Going for the Bronze
メダルコース　【改訂新版】フルカラー
ISBN978-4-523-25153-8 C7082

CD Book　各定価（本体1,000円＋税）

同時通訳の神様　國弘正雄先生推薦!!
東進ハイスクール　安河内哲也先生大推薦!!
Google日本法人元社長　村上憲郎氏おすすめ!!

真の実力は基礎に宿る!!
史上最高のコラボ完成!!

安河内哲也×英単語ピーナツ

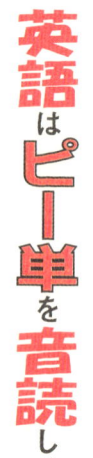

センター試験からやり直しまで

英語はピー単を音読しろ！

英単語ピーナツ **BASIC 1000**

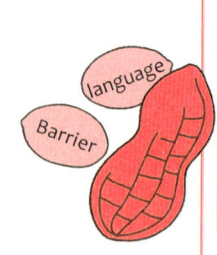

CD Book

安河内哲也
佐藤誠司　共著

● 英語学参・語学書
● 四六判／280ページ

ISBN978-4-523-25156-9 C7082　　定価（本体980円＋税）